MW00768373

Pandemic Survivor

Victim to Victor

God Bless You!
Thanks!

Eleanor George

Eleanor D. George

5/17/23

Unless otherwise indicated, all scripture references are from
Easy Standard Version (ESV)
King James Version (KJV)
Amplified Version (AMP)
Contemporary English Version (CEV)
Christian Standard Bible (CSB)

Pandemic Survivor: Victim to Victor
Copyright © February 2023
Eleanor D. George
ISBN# 978-1-953526-45-8

All rights reserved under international copyright law. This book or parts of thereof may not be reproduced in any form, stored in a retrieval system, or transmitted in any form by any means; electronic, mechanical, photocopy, recording, or otherwise without prior written permission of the publisher or author, except as provided by United States of America copyright.

Published by TaylorMade Publishing
Jacksonville, FL
www.TaylorMadePublishingFL.com
(904) 323-1334

TaylorMade Publishing

Table of Contents

Forward

In this incredible time in our society in the western culture, where we have been seduced into believing we have the power to reshape our reality into whatever form suits us, it is refreshing to find individuals with the courage to take a hard stare at the core of their inner person, and instead of searching for the quick fix, and the superficial make over, opt to begin the hard work of tearing down for the purpose of building up. This kind of personal renovation requires not only the willingness to initiate such a project, but also the determination to gain understanding as to what, where and how to proceed in this life changing process.

Eleanor George is such a person, who after many wrong turns going off the on ramp, is willing to share her journey in the beautiful lyrical fashion that only a truly gifted individual would dream to attempt. As you move through this work, you will share both pain and healing, and defeat turned to victory. As Eleanor continues her spiritual journey with a keen eye for the prize you will find her transparency is an invitation to the reader to join her in daring to dream for a life of change and conquest. It is a call to look inward with an honest eye, but to do so while acknowledging the presence of God that will insure the success of the enterprise.

Eleanor's success in sharing with you this writing, is a testimony to all of us that "we can do all things through Christ, which strengthen us."

Bishop Carlton T. Brown, DMin, D.D.
Senior Pastor/Chairman
Bethel Gospel Assembly, Inc.
New York, NY

i

Introduction

The success and feedback from my first book, "From the Heart, Poetry Birthed from the Altar of Life," made me realize my voice could continue to bring hope and healing to a victimized, traumatized and abused world. This second book was written for ordinary people who have felt stuck in a maze of disappointment filled with broken promises, broken-heartedness, poverty, and deferred dreams, and those who have felt lost and trapped in a pit of depression and inability.

I wrote this book to tell everyone it is not too late to pursue and realize your destiny; however, it will not be fully realized without the grace, love, intervention and power of God. I am a victor for one reason and one reason only, "Jesus loved me," and his love always "showed up." God was with me with each breath I took. God was with me in the darkest hours of my life. God tenaciously held me and would not let me go. His love and grace pursued me until He captured me in His everlasting arms. His mercy completely and gently quieted the enemy's shouts of condemnation and insignificance.

I pray that some word in this book will encourage you to see yourself as an overcomer – valuable and deeply loved – despite life's circumstances, experiences, destructive words from others or your choices. So, if you are reading this book, we have one important, invaluable thing in common – we are pandemic survivors! Think about it. You are alive today. Your past can remain in the pre-COVID world with everything else that is no more. You have been given a unique opportunity for transformation and transition. No one has to remain chained to victimhood or a negative past. You are a survivor! You are victorious! You are triumphant through Jesus Christ!

We can all move forward from a victimhood existence. Whether victimized by persons, places or systems, we are overcomers, conquerors, triumphant and victors through Christ and His love. I have survived a global pandemic to tell my story of hope, transformation and transition. Hopefully, I will inspire others to share and write their significant life's story as well. We have all survived the pandemic for

an important reason. Each of us has purpose, destiny and a future. However, without a personal relationship with Christ you will not be able to realize all that the Creator had in store when He made you.

Pandemic Survivor...Covid-19

Covid-19 was responsible for over 500,000 deaths in America within one year. This was the greatest loss of life ever experienced by Americans. It surpassed the death toll of the first pandemic in 1917 and World War I +. Our country and world were in a panic and fear which permeated every echelon of society. No one was exempt. Covid-19 was an equal opportunity killer. Scientist tried and researched but for months could not get a handle on this virus and human death continued. The medical community also experienced death rates that have been unprecedented.

The word "unprecedented" was uttered throughout the pandemic with each statistic. Schools closed, businesses closed, stores, theatre everything in cities and countries around the world were ghost towns as everyone shut in and sheltered in place to preserve life and stop the spread. All of the go-to sources, science, medicine, that usually had answers came up wanting. The greatest minds on the planet were baffled as if Covid-19 was an alien from outer space, like something out of the twilight zone. No one on this planet could stop this virus only partially contain it, or as they said, "mitigate the spread" at least for the moment. Everybody thought they could possibly die. We feared each other and the virus, like "the plague" – because it was a plague.

On January 2, 2021, I was diagnosed with that deadly disease. But in the midst of that storm, no - stage 5 hurricane-like storm, I was at peace. In the midst of Covid turmoil, I was at peace. How could I possibly be at peace being diagnosed with Covid 19? Would I end up on a ventilator gasping for each breath? I did not know. All I knew was that I was not alone. I was in the center of God's heart, my life was in his hands, and I was at peace. Jesus enveloped me with peace.

I went home, walked into my new kitchen, in my new home, only a month old, and declared, "God did not bring me into this new home to die!" Then, I laughed and laughed and laughed, not in delirium, but in truth, in the stated fact that I knew God had more for me. I knew that as the Bible said over and over and over, "And it came

to pass." And pass it did, within three weeks all symptoms ceased and desisted. I did not have to go to the hospital. I was not gasping for air on a ventilator. However, I did experience a fever of almost 102 and sometimes I felt a little labor to breathe. Abdominally there were issues, but I made it through - I survived! I was alive, only because of Jesus Christ. The vaccine came after…

So, today, I live to tell the story, but not only me. My son and daughter were both survivors of the deadly Covid-19. Consequently, these scriptures: "For in Him we live, and move, and have our being…" (Acts 17:28 NKJV) and "…And by His stripes, we are healed." (Isaiah 53:5 NKJV) became a reality, even more, in our lives. Sadly, that was not the case for so many others. Continually, my heart and prayers go out to everyone who lost a loved one…to Covid-19 and its variants.

Unfortunately, six months later in November 2021, after being fully vaccinated, I was told by my physician that I had sufficient antibodies and did not need the booster, in December 2021 I tested positive again for Covid-19 with the Omicron variant. My testimony is that the same God who sustained me the first time without life-threatening symptoms or hospitalization repeated His performance! This time I had even less severe symptoms than the first time – just a head cold with a small cough. Praise God – Whooohoo!

While I was quarantined and recovering the first time the notation of pandemics, I survived began to take shape. Consequently, during the second isolation and recovery, I completed the preliminary manuscript for this book! God opened my eyes to a new reality. I realized during these "bouts" that this "pandemic" was not the *only* "pandemic" that I have survived in my life. I was confronted with the fact that I had survived so many "pandemics" of tragedy, trauma, abuse and crisis.

Specifically, I survived the "pandemics" of abandonment, rejection, separation, being an orphan in foster care, adoption, incest, domestic violence, single parenthood, poverty, mental illness, wanting to die to escape misery, pain and substance abuse. Yes, I felt helpless and no one heard my screams because they were inside. But by God's grace, I survived!

I lived through the tragedies of broken relationships, toxic relationships, cycles and patterns that occurred over and over, but I survived. Consequently, for these pandemics only the vaccine filled with the love, hope and healing in the Blood of Jesus kept me alive. God made me a "Pandemic Survivor" to share my story so others can survive and eventually thrive – like I have.

Intimacy in a Pandemic

Isolation Victim

Isolation was a huge issue during the COVID-19 pandemic. For people who lived alone and for those who lost loved ones, it was like being on an emotional ventilator – gasping for the breath of fresh air brought into our lives by relationships that were gone. Many were left alone to deal with life, deal with this pandemic, deal with an empty home, apartment or room without the presence of a loved one, without intimacy. So, what happens when you find yourself living alone, not in a relationship with a significant other, hearing only one human voice – yours?

I was alone in my apartment without the comfort of a human presence. I ended a toxic relationship in June 2020, during the height of the COVID-19 pandemic. That first night, I gave myself permission to grieve the loss with tears and words. I allowed myself to feel the emotion, acknowledge it – but I also acknowledged the presence of God going through this emotional and physical loss with me.

Thankfully, God had prepared me for that moment months before it arrived. My relationship with God grew stronger as I spent more quiet time in prayer, reflection, and meditation on Him and his love as I read scriptures describing God's unconditional love for me. I was not unloved. I found love in which I was secure and safe. This love gave me the courage to make the final decision – sever.

When I prayed, I poured out my heart to God and held nothing back. In those moments of rawness something remarkable and wonderful occurred. The very presence of God filled my room, my heart, my body, my mouth, and my soul – God's presence. Many times, I would feel a trembling. Sometimes it was gentle and sometimes it was stronger – an enveloping warmth. At times I would even feel static electricity in the air. Other times it was like goose bumps on my skin.

But always, there was this sense that I was not alone, that there was a God who heard the cry of my heart and made His presence known – because He cared.

Now, you may not feel these strong sensations that I do; you may feel something different, or you may not "feel" anything at all – But God is still there. "The LORD is close to the brokenhearted and He saves those who are crushed in spirit." (Psalm 34:18 AMP) This was relationship – intimacy with a true and living God – not empty religion.

Even in an isolating "break-up" coupled with COVID isolation – "shelter in place" orders, quarantine, no visitors, broken and severed relationships due to COVID – even the death of loved ones (over one million Americans died), your heart does not have to die of loneliness! I am a witness that through the pandemics of isolation, aloneness and loneliness God showed up – with His presence and through scripture – daily.

Scripture after scripture, time and time again, as I turned to my Bible I would read God's love for me, an answer to a heartache, words of confidence in a God bigger than me, which told me that I am safe, secure, loved, that there is a future and a hope for me – even if I live alone, not in a special relationship, without a spouse, boyfriend or significant other, or in COVID isolation – I can still be a whole woman, a whole human being, completely fulfilled, fully loved – unconditionally. I can be intimate with the Lord God Almighty, my father, my shepherd, my friend, my Rock, to withstand any pandemic that is in my path on this journey called life.

Some of you may think this notion of intimacy with God is crazy. How can you be intimate with a God you cannot see, physically touch, or even audibly hear? There is the still small voice of God that you can hear with the ear of your spirit when you are in relationship with Him. God wants to be in communion with mankind. God wants to be in relationship with each human being He created. God wants us to

enjoy relationship and intimacy with Him – that was the reason God created mankind.

Why deny yourself the opportunity to be in intimate relationship with the Creator of the universe who says in the Bible, "every hair on your head is numbered," "every tear you cry is captured in a bottle by God," and that God knows your "down sitting and uprising." God knows everything about you. He knows what makes you happy and what makes you sad. Remember, He created you; you did not create yourself. You and I did not come from an ape or any other animal. We were created by a God who breathed life into us.

We are unique, different than any animal in the "wild kingdom." When I let God into my heart as an 11-year-old child, God made himself known to me. So, what about you? Is God making himself known to you? Are you experiencing the presence of God right now, as you read this sentence, this book? Do not harden your heart or ignore the Holy Spirit or the Word of God. "Now is the acceptable time." We learned a hard lesson in the pandemic, "tomorrow or the next second is not promised to you."

I survived the pandemics of loneliness and isolation, not only in the coronavirus pandemic but every "pandemic" in my life, through relationship with God through Jesus Christ.

Isolation Pandemic Survivor

I love God because He designed humans with the desire for communion with other human beings. God created Adam and Eve to commune and have fellowship and companionship. COVID-19 threatened the very core of humanity by robbing us of that communion. We were forced into separation, isolation and aloneness for survival.

But if you are a child of God, you are never alone. You have the presence of God in your space and you become part of the huge family of God. Through faith in Jesus Christ for salvation you are adopted into the "Body of Christ." You now have numerous brothers and sisters in

your life – through your church or fellowship. God also gave me special friends, brothers and sisters in Christ with whom I could share my deepest pain, hurt or problem – without judgment. As part of God's family, you share concern for each other.

As an only child, I felt a unique isolation and aloneness. But it does not have to be that way. One of the biggest benefits of salvation is your church family. God wants his children to fellowship and spend time together through prayer, Bible study, worship, enjoying food together, talking and laughing. During this pandemic, I communicated with my Christian family through phone calls, texts, emails, prayer conference calls, and video chats. I watched live streamed services every Sunday and Wednesday, where I could comment in the chat and read heartfelt comments from my brother and sisters in Christ.

During my bout with COVID, I began planning for my birthday and housewarming party. Despite the deadly virus, I had a virtual housewarming and birthday celebration on February 12, 2021. It was amazing, and I looked and felt beautiful and was extremely grateful to be alive and COVID free! We played "Name That Tune" on ZOOM (with the assistance of my amazing daughter, Dejshona) and had a dance and worship party – Whoohooo!

God opened up creative ways for his children to stay connected. None of us had to die emotionally or spiritually in isolation. My son, Michael, who captured this amazing birthday in a pandemic moment, which later became my Facebook profile picture for 2021 – Victory in a Pandemic, took the photo below!

Later, following CDC guidelines, I was able to physically fellowship in our house of worship, Bethel Gospel Assembly – Destiny Pavilion in the heart of Harlem, NY. I broke my isolation and aloneness and fellowshipped in a pandemic, despite fear of infection. I will be forever grateful for the ministers and worship team who courageously

and tirelessly served, sang, played instruments, prayed, exhorted and encouraged us during the pandemic.

Also, God kept his children busy by helping others during the pandemic. Our church provided food and clothing for the community throughout the pandemic – especially providing hand delivered meals and assistance for seniors and shut-ins. We also gave food for Thanksgiving and coats for Christmas to students in an elementary school in Harlem, thereby blessing numerous impoverished families.

Being part of the global Body of Christ has also given me a sense of belonging and purpose that counteracted feelings of loneliness and isolation, especially when we sent food, clothing and supplies to the Union Gardens community in Jamaica. We also sent live videos back and forth with them. Communicating, participating and engaging in national and international phone prayer lines, video calls and live streaming let me know that I could reach out and touch someone, even if it was through technology.

No one has to live in this world or go through their lives alone – we have each other, especially as Christians in the Body of Christ. We are each other's "keepers," especially in Christ. As I reach out by phone to the seniors in our church to see if they are alright or call a friend just to hear a human voice and they, in turn, hear mine, I am in relationship – no longer isolated. God has given me the strength to reach out, to give – but also to receive.

During the pandemic, many people shared food, assistance, encouragement, and love in so many forms. I am grateful that God made a way by using people, especially within the Body of Christ, to reach out to one another and allowed us to have human contact during that most difficult time.

The theme of this book is to acknowledge the pandemics of our lives while celebrating even the smallest victory along the way. My prayer is that you may see your life through different lenses, put your

past in perspective and gain hope in Christ for the present and any future pandemics that you will survive!

"For I know the plans I have for you," says the Lord. "They are plans for good and not for disaster, to give you a future and a hope." (Jeremiah 29:11 NLT)

Triumphant Survivor

The significance of my story has taken on a new urgency and relevance. I am a survivor of the coronavirus pandemic. I am also a survivor of a COVID-19 body invasion; I was diagnosed twice in 2021. The day after New Year's I had the initial deadly strain, and then on Christmas Day I was diagnosed with the Omicron variant, though I was fully vaccinated.

Even today, the world is still battling COVID-19 and its variants. I realized that God wanted me to share how I survived, not only COVID-19 but the numerous, deadly "pandemics" in my life.

Being sheltered-in-place coupled with quarantine periods afforded me unprecedented time to reflect on my life and update my story with a new perspective. As I emerged from my chrysalis of pandemic solitude, I understood why this manuscript has taken eight years until publication. Eight stands for New Beginnings, which is what my life has experienced during this entire pandemic-series of new normals and beginnings.

As you will read, so many wonderful events and personal understandings have emerged as I continually survived. My life is a testimony that despite any past or present experiences, we can endure, survive, thrive and emerge a beautiful, fully developed butterfly. We can complete the purpose, plans and destiny for our divine survival. That understanding brought an unrelenting hope in the face of challenges.

God had taken the "ashes" of my life and turned them into "beauty." Since Acts 10:34 declares, "God is no respecter of

persons…" God will do the same for you! No matter what you have been through, there is hope! You were created and you are special. No individual on the planet is insignificant or unimportant. But it is crucial that you begin to see your worth and value – you do not have to do it alone. God is with you. God will help you see yourself the way He sees you, "Fearfully and wonderfully made." (Psalm 139:14)

God calls you right now, "The apple of his eye." (Psalm 17:8) It was these scriptures that helped shape my identity and pull me out of a false and lost identity, where I felt unloved and insignificant. In the book of Genesis, the beginning, God said every part of His creation was "good." God's declaration included you and included me. Just the way we are – God has crazy love for us, His most precious creation.

Unfortunately, many people tend to be judgmental with themselves and others. They do not understand why people talk, act or think about themselves in self-degrading ways. Even the most talented, gifted, beautiful, prominent people have suffered from low self-esteem at some point in their lives.

But there is a reason for every action and reaction. There is a root under the plant. You may not see it, but the root is there. Unless we take the courage to begin to look at what is under everything, our feelings, words, behaviors and thoughts – the roots – we can go through a lifetime of imprisonment. We may be functional – but living in misery, torture and pain.

I thank God for helping me to take the journey to figure out "me." Now I am aware, when I say something, or react a certain way, what is at the root of the response. I can address the root cause and not judge myself by the symptoms. I am reminded that, "Who the Son sets free is free indeed!" (John 8:36)

Jesus Christ has set me free from the chains of my past. Now I live in today and tomorrow healthier, with a deeper appreciation and love for God, others and myself. I am still a work in progress – we all are – developing necessary boundaries while respecting others. But it

is great to know that I am *not* helpless, hopeless, incapable of change or inherently bad, which was the entrenched lie I believed for decades.

This journey to wholeness may not be a walk in the park. Quite the contrary, it may take painstaking inventory, tears and allowing yourself to be exposed – to you and God. This looking-in-the-mirror process of self-examination may conjure up difficult emotions and memories that were previously denied or hidden.

Sometimes I felt worse before I began feeling better. I was ensured that the pain associated with honesty and recovery was within the context of God's grace and love. So despite "whatever," I always knew I was safe in His arms and that God's spirit/presence and His word/scripture would not harm me. "For I know that plans I have for your saith the Lord, not of evil but of peace…" (Jeremiah 29:11)

However, there were many times that cycles of defeat left me feeling condemned, helpless and hopeless. I heard the unfortunate familiar lie in my ears, conceived through harsh words spoken externally or internally – this resounding, dismal, condemning, hopeless verdict, "Stop trying, you will never change!"

Nothing could have been further from the truth. "I can do all things through Christ that strengthens me*!*" (Philippians 4:13) It was true then and it is true now. For I can be transformed by the renewing of my mind, (Romans 12:2). God clearly showed me how all things *did* work together for my *good* in my life – no matter how horrific. (Romans 8:28) Being a constant work in progress, God showed me that change, transformation, being and living better was possible for me – instantly or over time.

Not surprisingly, I am a witness, that the journey to wholeness is possible and well worth the work and discomfort. As you embark on this journey with me, know that God will enable you to make it safely to the shore – even if on the broken pieces of our lives. (Acts 27:44) God knew how to take the broken pieces of my life and make a beautiful mosaic, bringing healing to the world. What God did for me,

He will do for you. Together, we can experience *all* of our ashes turned into joy!

"Pandemic Survivor," are you ready to move from being a victim to a victor? I know you are or you would not be reading this book! I celebrate your many victories and the ultimate victory you will experience if you dare to face you and all that you are – and dare to believe all you can become. Remember, there is no scripture that says, "God helps those who help themselves." God helps those who know they *can't* help themselves and instead rely on Him. Selah. It is OK to admit that you need help. As the old adage admonishes, "There is no cure for a sick man who thinks he's well."

I had to look to God, my highest power, who was bigger than my issues, situations and pain. In honesty I cried, "God if you are real, *help me* – I'm drowning!" What kept me alive instead of drowning in a depressive, no self-esteem-abyss-of self-hate-blame-shame-sea-of-despair was the Holy Spirit.

The Holy Spirit gently, but ever so profoundly, spoke the truth of scripture into my soul, "You are fearfully and wonderfully made." (Psalm 139:14) You are God's "workmanship." (Ephesians 2:10) God spoke to my soul, "I created you just the way *I* wanted to." Eleanor, when I created you, "It was good."

Similarly, you are unique and God has placed greatness inside of you – but sometimes it is covered by layers of "stuff" that suffocate and strangle the life God originally intended for you. I realized that I would have shrunk into oblivion had God not rescued me and revealed truth as He peeled back the grave clothes, like layers of an onion. Surprise! My authentic self was revealed, a butterfly with eagles' wings.

You, too, can soar! We all can soar and experience the joy of taking step after step as we reach toward victory and triumph! Victory *is possible* for you and me – if we dare to believe.

Victim to Victor

Abused, confused, self-destruct in 10 minutes…

Undelivered, bound, scared, crying, fear
Helpless, hopeless, discouraged, despaired
Lying, manipulative, pleasure seeking to relieve pain,
boredom, life feeling stalled...
Want to die, want to lie down…and never get up – Victim.

Victim of sexual, physical, mental abuse,
Victim of lies, deception, people, places, things
Finally – accepted Christ, but traces of fear and unbelief
sometimes lingered within like mildew, residue
birthing doubt, double mindedness and turmoil – led
To faithlessness, self-destruction, and loss of peace within
But, confession, honesty led to relationship restored.
Don't deserve it, none of us do – but "One More Time."

God forgave and rescued
The Light within brightened and restored…
To see the light of victory down the road,
Sometimes seemed so unattainable,
Self-became a stumbling block.
Then God whispered… "Peace Be Still…"

It's My plan, not yours.
I *will* perform My will.

"Make up your mind!" they say.
"Stop making excuses,"
"Do you really want to serve God,
Or appease self?" Despite unending criticism –

Still the gnawing at your soul,
Of a different you,
A better you,
An in control, whole, totally free you.
Help Lord, only you really understand…

Christ says Peace Be Still.
I see you praying, crying, longing to be free,
You will be free – but only in Me.

To me, that's Victory,
That's the victory I seek.
Victory not just over evil,
Not just Victory over me,

But Victory to *Trust* God.
To *Bring Me* Into Victory.

There is still hope.
Because there is still Christ.
Who beckons me – Come! I love you,
I died for you,
So that you can live in victory,
Over and over again,
I will take you from Victim to Victor,
Just hold My hand,
For I know the plans I have for you!
Everything will happen,
Just as I planned!
Trust me. I love you.
Trust me. I made you.
Don't let go of My hand.
Yes Lord…
Now I understand.

Victory Along the Way – The Process

The Journey Out of Victimhood

This book is not just about the finished product; it is about the victories we experience along our journeys. Victory comes not only when you finally reach your goal, but also, each step you take towards your goal of emotional and physical wholeness, security and healthy self-love – is victory. Each and every victory in our lives has significance. We become victors each time we become aware, identify and begin to make steps to authenticity.

We can discover a healthy, loving, safe place within ourselves – despite our past or what life brings our way. Victory is not a destination but a continuum. Therefore, we can experience victory along that continuum. We can experience victory in the middle. Some of the greatest moments I have shared with God happened in the middle of a situation, while I was going through, during the difficult moments when the end seemed so far off. I have learned to cherish being in the middle, because that is where I began to really learn God and myself.

This knowledge of such a wonderful, good, I-will-never-leave-you-or forsake-you God, infinite in power, wisdom and love propelled me to not quit or give up – but to keep moving, step by step, until I made it through to the end. There was victory in the middle. As I once heard and read in T.D. Jakes "Crushing" (book and videos), you cannot have victory without first being a victim. Believe it or not, being a victim can be the first step to victory for you, your family, community, nation and world for generations.

Imagine leaving a legacy of survival, victory, overcoming obstacles, pushing through pain, learning to lean on Jesus the entire way as God's loving compassionate hand moved you from victim to victor. That's my story – and I am still in the victory making process, which does not end until I reach the pinnacle of my dreams, heaven's

spectacular, awesome, amazing, glorious and well-worth-it-no-matter-what-I-had-to-go-through-in-life-to-reach shores!

This literary journal began pre-pandemic when I was in my 50's, however the culmination of this book came during one of the worst global pandemics in the history of mankind. I am now in my very early, youthful 60's, (the new 40's) recently retired after more than 20 years of elementary and middle school teaching in one of the roughest areas in the country, New York City.

I spent my entire career living in the Bronx community of my students, teaching numerous underrepresented students of color born in America who were not living the "American Dream," but its nightmare. I also taught children of immigrants from a myriad of cultures, who spoke various languages.

I have seen the best of life and the worst of life living in one of the greatest cities in the world. Life in the Bronx and New York City mirrored life across the country. Tragically, America remained "a Tale of Two Cities." As Charles Dickens coined in his timeless book, "It was the best of times, it was the worst of times." However, in the "tale of two cities" of my own journey – Christ has been the constant anchor that brought sanity and hope into desperate, traumatic, hopeless and chaotic situations.

There were unfruitful days and unfulfilled seasons in my life. My soul became thirsty for a drink of the cool waters of security, sanity, peace, joy, providence and relief from the disparity, injustice, inequity, even insaneness of my choices, trauma, pain and hurt that the human condition brought within a dichotic society.

I desperately reached for so many things to fill that thirst and hunger of my soul. But I have learned through experience that what I reached for only provided temporary relief – not true satisfaction. Only when I drank from the well of Jesus Christ and ate the Bread of Life did I enter fulfillment. When I allowed Jesus to completely fill my soul,

the yearning of my heart was quenched. I was no longer empty, nor was my inner-woman soul void.

My journey to the center of fulfillment occurred within a cultivated relationship with Jesus Christ. I had to "taste and see that the LORD was good" for myself. Consequently, I learned that "blessed is the man (or woman) that trusts in him." (Psalm 34:8) It is safe to trust Christ with yourself. God will not destroy or annihilate you but restore, renew and reconstruct your life. This is the truth. "God is not man that He should lie…" (Numbers 23:19).

It has taken a lifetime for this truth to become part of my being, through various experiences with God, faith, belief and the devastation of doubt and unbelief. Today after over six decades of existence filled with sunshine and rain, hard defeats and exquisite victories – I have come to one conclusion. Jesus *is* Love and He loves *me*. Jesus is *my* omniscient, quenching Living Water. Jesus is *my* omnipotent Bread of Life. Jesus is *my* ultimate and only omnipresent Hope. Only the Lord Jesus Christ can entirely fill the empty, parched and starving soul with an unconditional fountain of unending, dependable, trustworthy, committed, secure, love, peace, hope and joy.

I finally learned, understood and fully believed Jesus' daily invitation to "Come" found in Isaiah 55:1-2 (KJV), "*Ho, everyone that thirsteth, come ye to the waters, and he that hath no money; come ye buy and eat; yea, come, buy wine and milk without money and without price. Wherefore do ye spend money for that which is not bread? and your labour for that which satisfieth not? hearken diligently unto me, and eat ye that which is good, and let your soul delight itself in fatness.*"

When I accepted Christ's invitation of love to "Come," my soul found delight in "full, fat love" not leanness, withholding or scarcity love. In Christ, I have found the love my heart and soul was thirsty for. This love began, as Jeremiah said, "in my mother's womb." God knew me and called me. But I did not know it – until I believed. You, too, can hear His call and know His love.

"Hey there! All who are thirsty,
come to the water!
Are you penniless?
Come anyway—buy and eat!
Come, buy your drinks, buy wine and milk.
Buy without money—everything's free!
Why do you spend your money on junk food,
your hard-earned cash on cotton candy?
Listen to me, listen well: Eat only the best,
fill yourself with only the finest.
Isaiah 55:1-2 (MSG)

What have you experienced throughout your journey? What information did you learn about yourself? What did you get out of each experience, good or bad? What life lesson did you learn, or had to keep experiencing until you learned? One thing I noticed is that God allowed me to experience the same test, the same monkey wrenches in my life and my relationships until I saw the unhealthy patterns and cycles. God waited until I was exhausted, surrendered and submitted to his love and guidance. God waited until I was ready to listen – without argument. Faith and trust gave me the courage to begin the process of healing and thinking about things differently in order to have different results. As Einstein stated, "Insanity is doing the same thing over and over but expecting different results." We live in a world of insanity – sometimes internally.

It is possible to live, grow and learn what triggers negative emotions and thoughts that result in self-defeating and harmful actions. This occurred in my life, especially when romantic relationships ended and emotional and physical suffering manifestations began. More times than not, those cyclic relationships triggered reactions of increased grief and sorrow in my life.

I felt powerless as my life spun out of control. Hitting the same brick wall, over and over again, not only left me with a headache, but also led to heartache and frustration, causing me to turn on myself.

Ultimately, I felt hopeless, helpless, defeated and varied degrees of depression. Sometimes, in desperation, I tried to manipulate or control situations and people in hopes of a better outcome – only to be trapped again deeper in darkness.

During this process, I discovered, especially in interpersonal relationships, that when an action or word triggered abandonment, the mental, emotional and behavioral downward spiral began. This spiral was fueled by feelings of rejection that triggered insecurity, feeling insignificant, and thrown away which then triggered me to feel threatened or unsafe. This would be evident in self-defeating self-talk, and sometimes, irrational behavior, which then triggered the self-blame cycle that continued over and over inside my head. This emotional/spiritual cycle robbed my sleep, peace, health and contentment. Sound familiar? You are not the only one.

The first step was to admit there was a problem. Then I needed to identify the cycle(s). What was going on? What triggered each stage of demise? Tough questions, but with the aid of the gentle Holy Spirit enveloping me in love, I pursued my own truth.

Next, I asked God to reveal the root of all this insanity as I dug and dug. The process was not accomplished overnight. It took years of self-evaluation, examination and inventory to find the root. God showed me habitual negative patterns and cycles in my life. God also clarified what triggered these patterns and cycles.

Additionally, I began to notice certain idiosyncrasies and tendencies in my personality. It became apparent that when triggered, I had problematic go-to and knee-jerk reactions. Often, the human psyche uses these insane behaviors and patterns as "barriers" to protect ourselves – even though they ultimately perpetuate hurt and pain.

This part of my process continued over time – issue by painful issue – identifying root causes, triggers and my reactions. Once that was accomplished, another step in the victory process was reaching out for help and beginning the work of identifying the personal steps

needed to break the unhealthy patterns and cycles and live a healthier life – especially internally. I reached out to confidential small group settings and interventions that dealt with trauma and abuses both sexual and physical mostly held at my local church as well as with trusted ministers, both male and female. I also reached out to organizations such as Milagros Day Worldwide, turning "abuse to success" which ultimately gave me a platform to fulfill my purpose as a writer.

Ultimately, my Bishop Carlon T. Brown of Bethel Gospel Assembly, sponsored my books, "From the Heart Poetry Birthed from the Altar of Life," for the 30 domestic violence/trauma survivors who completed the Milagros Day Worldwide leadership "Bootcamp" retreat. We dealt with issues surrounding domestic violence, sexual and physical abuse, and trauma-filled childhoods and discovered (or confirmed) our purposes as leaders – not only survivors. Towards the end of the retreat we created individual vision boards. It was an amazing life-changing experience. This was all part of coming out of victimhood into *victor*-hood as I was exposed to thriving, not just surviving.

I learned, along with others, that abuse did not define me; it was my story – not my identify. But it was through Christ that I learned my identity, that I was "fearfully and wonderfully made." Throughout the process, God allowed me to meet people, especially women, who experienced much of the same trauma, abuse and issues as myself. I received comfort and I learned to comfort others with the comfort and help that God showed me.

It humbled me to realize that God used *every* experience in my past to help someone else – to liberate, empower and reinforce each person's God-given significance. I remember what it felt like being alone, dejected, isolated in pain, insignificant and ashamed. But I have also tasted freedom and success. I have experienced that deliverance and transformation is possible. "Faith is the evidence of things not seen the substance of things hoped for" which became my new reality – over time.

Notice, I continually use the word "victory." Even when in the "victor making process," I sometimes felt like a victim and defeated. This occurred especially as I experienced setbacks or relapsed into old familiar thought and behavior patterns.

However, each step taken by faith in the journey to wholeness and freedom was still considered a victory. I *could* have tragically lived my whole life in denial and never taken personal inventory. I *could* have indefinitely accepted and lived with unconscious destructive patterns and reactions to life and people. Far too many people remain in victimization, beneath their purpose, for a lifetime – sometimes because it seems too difficult and frustrating to change. But once we begin to see ourselves as better, and visualize taking the first baby steps towards healing, breaking patterns and ultimately transformation – we can regain hope. We can be gentler and kinder with ourselves and ultimately with others. This alone is a *huge* victory and must be celebrated.

We were like babies taking our first steps as our heavenly Father looked on with pride, pleasure, and love and encouraged us to take our next step(s). We were not alone in this process – we are never alone. Our Father, the Lord God Almighty – the Highest Power – is with us! God is there to pick up the pieces of our brokenness and put as back together better than new – transformed.

When you see the title "Victim to Victor," victory was not simply a destination but a theme throughout the ups and downs of my life. During the pandemic I saw God continue the process of moving me from victimhood into victory. I survived testing positive for COVID-19 twice in one year, despite two underlying conditions that could have resulted in severe sickness and death. I am alive to tell the story of God's healing and sustaining power.

In addition, in the midst of the pandemic, God kept me employed – even saving money. In this pandemic, by God's grace, providence and open doors, I purchased my first cooperative unit, brand

new, with a terrace and an amazing view – which was a desire of my heart. I moved from renting to owning – all during a pandemic!

While sheltering-in-place I had the courage to finally end a dead-end relationship, made personal decisions about my relationship with God and myself that changed the trajectory of my life – all during a pandemic. I began to realize that God had brought me through many pandemics in my life, which will be discussed in this book.

After taking my own personal inventory I began to endlessly write about each discovery in my journal. I wrote about each tear, pain, hurt, revelation, success and victory. I wrote about each time I overcame and each time I experienced relapse. I was in recovery, recovery from a suffering self, living below the wonderful standards God set for his children. Eventually these thoughts, steps and reflections led me to my computer, where I typed and worked out many of my understandings. Sometimes I was at my keyboard from midnight until daylight. This ultimately led to the writing and completion of "Pandemic Survivor: Victim to Victor."

Before I go any further, I would like "you" the reader to pause. You are also a pandemic survivor. Take full advantage of this time of reflection. Quiet yourself and your inner voice. Ask God to help you to see not only the defeats in your life – but the many victories. These victories along the way are stepping-stones to wholeness, to finally breaking free from old destructive patterns and creating and/or adopting new healthier patterns.

Through these moments of reflection (and journaling) you can develop better, positive ways of thinking and speaking about and to yourself. This discussion and exercise is needed today. People can feel like trapped failures without a "clue" or strategy to begin the process of breaking cycles in their lives. Therefore, I am sharing some of my experiences so you can gain hope – that there is a way out of the craziness that plagues our minds and lives.

One important note: My relationship with God has been my lifeline, especially, when I could not believe in my ability to change during *momentary* failures. This relationship has kept me from suicide, total depression, completely giving up or living in the psychiatric ward as a regular customer. My prayer is that you may experience a relationship with Christ that helps you work through and unravel the layers of the "onion" of insidious issues that lie within.

Throughout the pages of this book, you will find those scriptures that were crucial in my development – as well as calming my fears, feelings of rejection, abandonment and ultimately healing. God's word shut up the voices that screamed "abandoned," "rejected" and "unloved." God's word declared I was "accepted in the beloved" and "I will never leave you or forsake you," and "I called you by name, you are mine" – I belonged.

God also restored power, authority and dominion that was lacking in my life. You are not the only one and you are not alone. The same God who transformed me is willing and able to love you into transformation, victory and triumph! For me, that is victory – to help others experience transformation, victory and triumph in their own lives.

Fasten your seat belts – you are in for the ride of your life!

"I chose you before I formed you in the womb;
I set you apart before you were born.
I appointed you a prophet to the nations…"
(Jeremiah 1:5 CSB)

"The Spirit of the Lord God has taken control of me!
The Lord has chosen and sent me
to tell the oppressed the good news
to heal the brokenhearted and
to announce freedom for
prisoners and captives…"
(Isaiah 61:1 CEV)

My Story - The Beginning...

"For I know the plans and thoughts that I have for you,"
says the Lord,
"Plans for peace and well-being
and not for disaster
to give you a future and a hope."
(Jeremiah 29:11 AMP)

It all began on February 12, 1960, in Queens, New York.

♫ "It was a very good year…" ♫

I was born and named Victoria Scott.

I did not know who my biological parents were. I did not know the circumstances of my birth or why I was put up for adoption. It was left up to me to make meaning of my tragic, unfortunate, not-my-fault-but-I-always-felt-that-somehow-it-was, traumatic, shameful truth of being orphaned/adopted.

Eventually I buried it deep inside – so deep that it left my consciousness. I made myself forget and lived identity-less. My biological parents' names, faces and history were a mystery to me because the adoption was closed and the records were sealed. All I remember from my earliest childhood was my pink bunny that gave me comfort and security.

In late adulthood, I came across the agency's notes from the early months of my life. The notes said I came to the orphanage with my pink bunny. I realize now that my attachment to the bunny resulted from the thought that the cuddly toy could be from my natural mother and it was my only connection to her and her love. I am sure at some level we bonded, but I was separated, severed from her scent, the warmth of her body, her embrace, her smile, and her love. I was left

alone as a crying baby when I should have been safe, secure and snuggled in my mother's arms. I was born, orphaned, and entered foster care – abandoned but thank God, eventually adopted by two wonderful parents in 1961, Alphonso and Anna George.

From my inception, I have been dealing with issues that have ripped through my self-esteem and identity and left me with a lingering sense of insecurity, insignificance and being unwanted – as well as shame. Unfortunately, I did not identify or verbalize this until five decades later. This is the backdrop for the life of a beautiful, amazing, resilient, talented woman – me. The curtain has opened and Victoria Scott, renamed Eleanor Denise George, emerged on the stage of life. Will it be a tragedy, comedy, mystery or thriller? Would there be a happy ending or one filled with sorrow, tears and death? Only time would tell the tale.

It took almost a year to complete my adoption. Then, I was renamed Eleanor Denise George and taken to my new home, new family and new life. Let me pause here. Through my adoption, I lived the salvation story that I would experience years later. At salvation, the Lord Jesus Christ redeemed me, I became born again, and my sins were totally and completely forgiven by God. When I received Christ into my heart, I became adopted into the family of God, the Body of Christ. Then I was renamed from sinner to saint, from lost to found. I was redeemed and reconciled as a reborn child of God.

Decades later, while taking a class at my local church, I had the opportunity to learn the meaning of my first, middle and last names – it was eye opening to say the least. Eleanor is Greek and means "enlightenment." Denise is a French name, which means "believer." George is also Greek and means "tiller of soil or cultivator." As my life unfolded, all of these names became significant regarding my identity, personality, talents, abilities, gifts, strengths and God's divine purposes for my life.

I was my parents' only child – their baby girl – and they loved me dearly. They provided for me in ways that were almost unimaginable. Their provision went well beyond my basic necessities – they exposed me to the good of life and opportunities that most of my peers did not enjoy, as I later observed.

That should have been the end of the tragedy, a happy ending, once abandoned now adopted. I should have been safe and secure in a happy home, to grow up into a well-adjusted, balanced woman full of self-worth. I should have lived, "happily ever after." However, as time would tell, I faced mental health issues, physical and sexual abuse, domestic violence, drug abuse, single parenthood, public assistance and a litany of traumatic circumstances that would cause anyone to give up, crawl in a shell of fear and never come out or return to life.

But by the grace of God, after all I have been through; despite every abuse, God was there. He loved me, picked me up, and healed and restored me to continue on the wonderful journey that he created for my life – one that has been filled with valleys but also mountain peaks.

Identity Crisis Pandemic Survivor Lost and Found

Rooted in my abandoned beginnings, I never had a clear sense of identity. When I was told that I was adopted, I could not fully comprehend the meaning as a 12-year-old child. I remember feeling lost, fear, unbelief and what does this mean? I told two friends that I was adopted, neither one of them believed me. One best friend said, "You're lying Eleanor, you look just like your father!" The thought that I was adopted and not really Anna and Alphonso George's daughter was unbelievable. But I was part of a wonderful family who loved me, how could this be? Who do I really belong to? The last question echoed in my mind for a lifetime...

Thankfully, God's loving grace became more and more sufficient as time went on. For all I knew, God could have been protecting me from a horrible life with my natural parents that could have left me devastated or permanently destroyed and void a viable relationship with God. Plain and simple, they were *not* a part of God's plan and destiny for my life or for my good. God had great and wonderful plans for me and, He hand-picked the two people He knew would love and raise me into the phenomenal, grateful woman that I am today.

God's love placed me in the most wonderful family that any baby, child, adolescent, and adult could want. I was accepted and loved by my adoptive parents. In their home I lived the life of a well taken care of only child – like a "princess." So it was earth shattering when I learned the truth...

So, one day I was told that I was an adopted child by my parents. My mother had a medical encyclopedia. She had a place held in the book on the page with the vocabulary word "adoption". She told me to read it while she and my father looked on. Then, she gently told me that I was adopted. I could hardly believe what I was hearing. Do

you mean that Anna and Alphonso George, who I believed all of my life was my two loving parents and who I derived my identity, were not my "real" parents? That I did not really belong to them from birth. That there was someone else who was my "real" mother and father? That they put me up for adoption in an orphanage? This event got translated into my young soul that "they" (my birth parents) got rid of me, that I was unwanted, but worst of all that I had no identity.

Tragically, the negative belief was planted that there must have been something so inherently wrong with me that "they" threw me away. I internalized the insidious lie that I must be really bad inside, which reinforced the bad feelings inside from being molested as a young child by an uncle. I already knew I was bad or doing something wrong, when sex was forced into my young life. Now, I knew for sure that I was so bad and disgusting that even my own natural mother did not want me.

All of these beliefs were born that day and festered for decades even after I accepted Christ. Painfully, after two days of living with that shocking news, it felt like I fell off the planet. My whole world was fake and crumbling around me. I was falling into a bottomless pit, a hopeless pit of rejection, abandonment, loss of identity, and destruction. The truth that I previously believed about myself, my family and my world was a lie! Did that mean that my cousins were not really my cousins? Did they know? Did the family know? I was told I was born with a different name. Who named me? Who was my mother? Who was my father? Why did they abandon me? Why couldn't they keep me and raise me and let me know them or where I came from? Who do I look like my mother or father? What do they look like? Their faces, smiles, personalities – all unknown. Didn't my mother miss me?

That is why my relationship with God became so important, because when my birth parents (or anyone) threw me away, there was a God who picked me up and loved me".

"When my father and my mother forsake me, Then the Lord will take me up." (Psalm 27:10 KJV)

Abandonment – Adoption

God, I feel so alone.
Why do I always end up in this place?
Abandoned and left alone,
And filled with excruciating pain and internal strife.
Rejection from a man triggered familiar
abandonment in my heart.
Why did I even start?
Lord I can't take this anymore!
I feel so abandoned,
So unwanted.
Love doesn't live here anymore.

From my birth abandoned
into an orphanage
A baby crying for her mother's love
– no response.
Her presence gone.
Bonded with abandonment.
How could she leave me?
Why didn't she want me?
What was wrong with me?
So wrong with me that she had to leave me?
Unconsciously buried was the thought
My birth was a mistake…
Was I a mistake?
Was my life a mistake?
Was I simply an unwanted mistake?

But God with His spirit of Adoption
picked up this helpless baby in His
everlasting arms
From my birth declared,
I want you.

I love you.
You are not a mistake.
I wanted you born
And your birth was my joy…

You will be adopted not only by Me and My love,
But I will give you two of the best parents,
And place you in their care.
I have created them to love you,
nurture you, raise you.
Ordained to love you from above,
throughout your childhood, adulthood and beyond…

Daughter now do you understand?
Also,
Daughter, I wanted you to know,
Your children always wanted you
Always loved you,
From the first moment of their birth
and will love you
Until the day you die.

Daughter, I have placed love in your life,
Be secure in Me.
Stop the inner turmoil,
Let my love stop your soul's inner strife.
You are wanted by Me and them...

Through salvation as a child.
You were adopted once again,
into the family of God.
Again you were adopted,
This time into My church.

My heart, My love
Will reside within My people.
My church will accept everyone

who walks through My doors.
Those who loved Me accepted
and loved you,
As you grew into a woman from a child.

You, once abandoned and forsaken,
Are now adopted and completely loved,
Once you accepted My invitation of love
to come into your heart,
You entered My solemn covenant of
Eternal adoption,
Eternal acceptance,
I want you; I want you, I want *you*…

You are loved!
You are My beautiful creation from above.
Do not worry about those who don't care and
who have forsaken you,
I never will.
"For I will never, leave you or forsake you"
You can rely on My love.

Again,
Let Me reassure you,
You never have to feel abandoned or forsaken,
My love will stay around.

Remember, even at your birth,
And the birth of so many other infants
that were in your shoes,
When mother and father abandoned you
I took you up!
I will always love you…

Remember
You have Me inside you
to forever be your company.

You are wanted, so wanted,
always wanted.

You have never been alone,
I have always been there
and
I will always care.

Love,
Jesus

Orphaned/Foster/Adopted Child Pandemic Survivor

Breaking the Bonds and Deliverance from these Viruses:

- Abandonment
- Rejection
- Identity Crisis
- Fear
- Shame
- Condemnation
- Lasting Guilt
- Self-Hatred
- Rebellion
- Depression
- Suicidal Thoughts
- Anger
- Bitterness

Vaccine – Finished Works of Jesus Christ through death, burial and resurrection, Name of Jesus, Blood of Jesus – coupled with forgiveness, love, acceptance and hope.

Adopted children live in a unique pandemic – which they did not cause and cannot control. A biological mother put them up for adoption – permanent separation – giving up her rights as a mother to the baby she grew for nine months and delivered into the world – thereby providing the opening for demonic forces to enter into the adopted infant or child's soul at the onset of separation.

This is also true for infants and children placed into foster care as they are separated from their parents. This is the pandemic of abandonment and rejection that the infant and adult must survive. Unfortunately, many adopted children continue to be infected by the

viruses of abandonment and rejection for the rest of their lives. These viruses simultaneously infiltrate the soul of the foster care child, even when adopted.

This pandemic of infant abandonment and rejection wreaked emotional havoc in the life of this infant – me. I was in an orphanage and foster care as an infant – the impact reverberated with ripples like a stone hurled into a peaceful lake. I was tortured in relationship after relationship. Rejection, abandonment, and separation were driving behaviors that led to further destruction throughout adulthood.

Abandonment and rejection infiltrated the soul, trying to devour the host, along with the viruses of shame, condemnation, guilt, no self-worth, and rebellion – rebellion against the God and family that let this happen. I experienced destructive forces that fueled the spirit of witchcraft – control by manipulation – born through rebellion fueled by pain and many times expressed in co-dependent tendencies. (1 Samuel 15:23)

There are numerous journals, articles and books about this subject and the effect of adoption on the adopted child, even into adulthood. However, my account does not come from any book, but from what I experienced as an adopted infant, child, adolescent, young adult and now as a mature woman. This is real. Additionally, if the various demonic forces coupled with negative behaviors and beliefs are not: 1) identified, 2) bonds broken through the finished work of Jesus Christ, in the Name of Jesus through the Blood of Jesus and 3) covered with God's forgiveness, love and acceptance – freedom becomes elusive.

By living in denial, one may appear to be outwardly successful, but deliverance and cessation of the internal torture and attacks will not occur without transparency. I have learned that the "skeleton" loses its power once you open the door. Had it not been for my relationship with Jesus Christ, I would be in such a tortuous, hopeless, mentally imbalanced state that I would probably be in an institution, in jail for

murder or in a cemetery – not writing this book for you, sharing the victory and deliverance along my journey.

You can be honest with Christ. Even if you are tortured to the point of denial with defense mechanisms enacted or involved in substance abuse for relief and ability to face another day – you are not alone. Even if you engaged in reckless behavior, co-dependency, avoidance, displacement, manipulation for self-preservation or you are filled with anger, rage, resentment, bitterness – internal agony – you can and will be delivered if you let Jesus Christ into the middle of your pain. There is relief. There is hope!

I am delivered from the agony and set free, even though it took time, success and seemingly failures and setbacks. What pulled me out of the pit was a soul deep belief, revived by the Holy Spirit, that Jesus really loved me, all of me. Also, that my birth brought God joy and that God's creation of me was inherently good, not bad. Lies were confronted by truth. Ultimately, the truth that Jesus died for my freedom emerged internally, in the middle of despair. God revealed through Christ that all my issues of abandonment, rejection, fear, loss of identity, shame, guilt, self-hatred, anger, rage, codependency, rebellion, manipulation, no self-worth, and peacelessness, was hung up on the cross with Jesus and destroyed by his shed blood.

Christ did this not only for me, but for everyone. All the issues of life that have plagued you internally and externally – that have kept you bound to torture and destruction – can be annihilated by Jesus' Blood, God's Word and ultimately, the full expression of God's love towards you. "He heals the brokenhearted and binds up their wounds." (Psalm 147:3) You are valuable to God. You are significant to God. God rejoices over you. God has wonderful plans for your life. God wants you to continue breathing. God wants you alive and wants you to experience true, complete freedom. It is possible. It is not too late. You can heal and be free. My life is not only a witness and a testimony of God's ability to heal, deliver, free, transform and cause every negative experience to turn out for my good – but God kept me alive

when I self-destructed and wanted to die. I remember when internal pain, grief, feeling sorry for myself, anxiety and hopelessness became my portion each day of my life, for a season. Thank God, those days are no more!

In time, everything negative became less and less and I healed more and more. In Christ, I became a new person, a healed and whole person. What God did for me, he can do for you, because God is "no respecter of persons." Listen to my story; hear God's voice in my deliverance. God will speak to you – if you let Him.

Abandonment, Adoption, Awareness and Healing – Identity Found

All I know about the circumstances of my birth is I was put up for adoption, which meant to me that I was rejected by my mother. The enemy then planted the lie that if my own mother gave me up, there must be something inherently wrong with me. I was never enough in my own eyes. This also birthed feelings of insignificance, despite the fact I was eventually adopted.

I always sought approval from my parents and other important figures in my life, including friends, family, teachers, employers and especially romantic relationships. It became familiar to minimize myself, point out my own flaws and wallow in the misery of self-rejection, insignificance and inadequacy. It took years for me to dig and connect the dots in my own life, but it was well worth the painstaking journey.

I never realized that being put up for adoption had triggered such deep feelings and had such an impact on my life and relationships. However, upon research I discovered that not only is a bond created between a mother and her fetus, but it is strengthened upon delivery. An infant knows exactly, biochemically, who their mother is. When that bond is broken by an infant being physically separated from their

birth mother, it triggers separation anxiety and deep-seated abandonment.

This cry for attachment being denied becomes the fabric of the infant, child, teenager, adult and mature adults being. It may lay dormant and hide deep inside until triggered by an event or separation from a significant person. I later discovered through therapy that during each break-up, I relived the tearing away and physical separation from my birth mother. In other words, I was constantly reliving separation, disconnection from my mother, anxiety, loss, grief, desperation and fear.

I learned that abandonment has many facets of impact and may present itself in different ways. I did not realize that quickly jumping into relationships was a way of me dealing with my abandonment. I tenaciously held on to someone who claimed they loved me. With each break-up, I experienced separation anxiety. I felt lost, alone and thrown away by my partner.

These negative feelings ultimately led to unbearable manifestations of anxiety that kept me locked into physical and emotional pain and rejection, which became a familiar and welcomed pattern. Sometimes, I would reject someone before they rejected me by breaking up with them, or not calling them. Then, the pain would become so intense that I would go right back to that person to avoid feeling alone and abandoned, even if they ignored me or treated badly.

The enemy used passive aggressive men to torture me into near insanity. The more I pushed, the more they pulled away and withheld love, affection and attention. Only Jesus Christ was able to break these cyclical negative relational patterns by filling my heart to overflowing with God's presence and love through the Holy Spirit.

There is hope for love to fill the deepest cisterns and wells of our hearts. I am accepted in the Beloved and God will never withhold love like others have. That is why forgiveness is also key to releasing the hurt and damage and moving into wholeness. With these

realizations, step-by-step, emotion-by-emotion, interaction-by-interaction I reminded myself that I am not abandoned or rejected. I spoke to these lies with the truth. I was accepted and loved by God. My identity was in Christ. I was a child of God and royalty. I was forever wanted – forever valued – forever loved.

Jeremiah 31:3b (NLT) declared, *"I have loved you with an everlasting love. With unfailing love I have drawn you to myself."*

Imagine a love that never fails – one that only God can promise and deliver. My worth and value is from a loving God, *not* a human being. Many times, I had to make myself think these thoughts to help counteract the negative thoughts and voices, especially condemnation. "There is therefore now no condemnation to them which are in Christ Jesus..." (Romans 8:1 KJV) Through God's word I received more tools in my toolkit to combat what previously had tried to destroy me. Those things became a stepping-stone to victory, triumph and testimonies of God's unfailing love that turned into this book!

There is only one message: Jesus loves you and me – for real and forever. That truth is why I believe in Jesus. This is why and how Christ has made the difference between life and death in my soul. With the knowledge deep in the crevices and chambers of my heart that I am *deeply, always loved by God*, I am triumphant – I cannot stay in hopeless despair! God always pulls me out of the pit with his unending love. I am grateful, filled with worship and praise for this truth about God and me. What about God and you?

Jesus is "touched with the feelings of my infirmity." (Hebrews 4:15) He knows better than any human being the trauma of abandonment. Because of our sin, Jesus experienced abandonment by his Father, when he cried out – as he was dying, being crucified on the cross of Calvary – "My God, my God why hast thou forsaken me?" (Matthew 27:46) Jesus alone bore my abandonment on the cross. He bore *all* your abandonment too – so we can be saved from utter despair and hopelessness. This is why the phrase "Jesus loves you and me" is

so meaningful and so complete. It is this love that has carried me and guided me through my journey for 62 years. However, my journey is not finished – I am still being processed. I am living in the "victor process" as I continually move from being a victim to a victor in each area of my life. Transformation, victory and triumph are possible – through the Lord Jesus Christ.

"Oh taste and see that the Lord is good, blessed in the man [or woman, or boy, or girl] that trusts in him." (Psalm 34:8)

Proverbs 31 Woman – Authentic Me!

(Seeing myself as God sees me...)

There was a time,
I only saw my flaws,
Looked down on a damaged self.

Loving myself I said with my mouth,
But deep in my heart there were,
feelings of worthlessness, anger and self-blame,
For all the trouble, shame, domestic violence and sexual abuse
I felt I allowed into my life.
And the negative-trying-to-cope-behaviors,
Only caused more strife.

So many times over and over,
Hurt myself with so many things,
Hoping to relieve the pain.
Wanting to love myself,
Sometimes – just didn't know how...

Even through becoming a believer,
Accepting Christ at the tender age of 11,
Not realizing how incest abuse
Had left deep impressions on my soul.
Filled me with guilt, shame, fear, petrified...

Even though it was not my fault.
Sometimes believed I was inherently bad,
Unaware of truth by a misguided self,
That God never looked down on me,
But only wanted to lift me up.

Domestic violence, mental illness,
Being exploited sexually over and over again,
Had made me feel like totally damaged goods.
Anger turned inward as I mutilated me,
Kept looking for love – in all the wrong places,
Even though love lived inside to set me free.
Jesus lived inside my heart,
And loved me from the start,
– but I had become too blinded by pain,
to see Jesus' love…for me.

Value lost; worth gone in a split-second suggested thought…
Insidious lies…
"There must be something so inherently wrong with you."
"So take what you can get!"
"Grab love wherever you can" … and I did.

As I read Proverbs 31 – the Virtuous Woman.
Over and over asking God
How can I ever be that woman with my past
and present?
I became shattered and broken,
Despite the masks of smiles and external confidence.

Until one day,
A sister in Christ told me,
You *are* the Proverbs 31 Woman!
God says you are.
Replace those negative words with God's words
About who you really are.
God loves you deeply beyond any man,

He wants to share this love with you always and forever.

He decrees you *are* worthy of His unconditional love.
God is crazy about you just the way you are,
So, lift your eyes above.

She admonished me to read Proverbs 31
In the mirror – everyday – to myself.
Quieting my soul in the presence of God
And put my name, Eleanor
Wherever a reference was made
To the Virtuous Woman –,

The Proverbs 31 Woman.

I cried and cried as the pain of decades began to leave my heart,
I read and spoke and looked at myself in the mirror.
I saw how God viewed me through,
His loving eyes,
And his amazing words about me.

Through this scripture and others,
God helped me to accept who I was
And reject who I was not.
No longer desperately seeking validation and love,
Because,
God enveloped me in unconditional love,
as I looked deeply into mirrored eyes.
I saw love stare back as a sparkle of light,
Helped me love and appreciate myself.
Believing how much He valued me,
Helped me value myself.
Believing how much He accepted me,
Helped me accept myself -
even if others did not.

God reminded me I was worth dying for!
I finally believed the worth and value
God deposited inside my soul,
Now I can live in authenticity.
Knowing I am His special, beloved daughter,
For all the world to see.
God said all he created was good…
That included me!

My birth was not a mistake.
Neither was yours.
You are a beautiful queen.
Created to give and receive love -
unconditionally.

I declare,
I am the Virtuous Woman in Proverbs 31
I am her and she is me.
Courageous, Resourceful, Beautiful, Dynamic, Powerful,
Capable, Praiseworthy, Phenomenal but most of all
Loveable, Beloved and
"The Apple of God's Eyes"
I am "Fearfully and Wonderfully made!"

I am the Proverbs 31 Woman!
And my Beautiful Sister so are you!

From Orphan to Queen

How your life begins does not determine your finale! On the stage of life, God can transform an orphan baby into a Queen. In the biblical book of Esther, we read about an orphan transformed into a Queen who ultimately saved her nation from annihilation. However, the transformation of Esther from orphan to Queen was a process.

First, she experienced being raised without her parents. She was orphaned, under the care of Mordecai, her Jewish cousin. Her birth name

was Hadassah, but she was renamed Esther in order to assimilate in Assyria – a foreign country that despised Jews and did not accept them as equals.

Although she was a natural beauty, Esther had to go through a specific preparation and development before she could be presented to the King as a prospective wife. Esther was not only beautiful, but also humble and gracious. Even in the palace, her character remained intact due to her relationship with God and godly counsel from her cousin. Though Esther experienced purposeful loss of identity, she eventually regained her authentic identity and heritage.

It is an amazing story, especially when she faced and accepted the reality of her Jewish identity and divine purpose. For a moment she shrank from her heritage, culture, identity and divine purpose in the King's palace. She kept hidden her identify for self-preservation. However, when she uttered the words, "If I perish, I perish but I'm going to see the King!" Esther finally lived in the moment of her ultimate purpose and identity – not just to be a beautiful Queen – but deliverer of her people. Her standing up for God and her nation resulted in their lives being spared. She spoke with integrity and authenticity and was able to influence a King.

Beyond the beauty and courage of this story about Queen Esther, I saw something I never realized. During a bible class, "Bad Women of the Bible" (bad meaning ultra-good, courageous, spectacular) our assignment was to study a woman in the Bible and draw parallels with ourselves. Although I fought the inward shrinking voice, "How dare you think of yourself as Queen Esther!" I was compelled to examine the similarities between Esther and myself. Just as Mordecai raised Esther, I was an orphan who was adopted and raised in a godly home. As did Esther, I lived in a world that many times did not value, love and respect my ethnicity or faith. Like Esther, I experienced the struggle with my identity at various points in my life. I also ran from my identify or adopted a false identify.

I also had to go through a sometimes painful refining, preparation and development process to become the woman God intended. However, like Esther, God had his hand on my life with divine purpose, destiny and beauty, inside and out. God pursued me and infused me with identity and purpose. God used me in my generation as his conduit of love to confront injustice, spiritual and emotional annihilation and to bring hope through personal conversations, transparent testimonies, public speaking, teaching, advocating social justice and especially writing. Therefore, as a Queen, a Pandemic Survivor, like Esther I am "in the kingdom for such a time as this."

There have been times in my life when I had to speak to power with integrity and authenticity- for example, at city council hearings, public forums with state officials, letters or emails to governmental agencies including the White House on various issues – or simply raising awareness. Our voices for justice, equity and integrity matter today as they did in the time of Esther thousands of years ago. The good news is when we stand for God and his justice, we never stand alone.

So, pandemic survivor you are alive, filled with purpose for a unique reason. I shared my experiences and awareness to jar personal reflection of *your* life. My hope is to point you to Jesus, to God, the Creator of "you" – to help connect the dots. Your life can save and rescue another life, your family, community, workplace, church and nation. We are alive to make a difference in this world. We are equipped to fulfill our divine purposes.

The Creator is always present – omnipresent to bring things to pass in our lives and the lives of others. Father, give us the faith to believe in You, Your power and Your plans for our lives. Help us to worship You as we help others and to be the phenomenal people You created us to be even "before the foundations of this world." Yes, all of us, like Esther, are alive "for such a time as this!"

It humbled me to even think that God had taken me as an orphan and developed (and continues to develop) me into a "Queen" with a powerful purpose for my generation and beyond. This revelation of God's conceptual identity and version of me has helped to break the identity lies of Satan to make me believe I was less than the phenomenal virtuous woman God created me to be.

God created me with value, worth, ability, gifts, talents and divine purpose. God created me – and all women – with the attributes of a Queen within. All I had to do was believe it, receive it, and envision myself as God saw me. Breaking the paradigm meant allowing God to transform my mindset and false identity that decades of life had cemented into core beliefs. As I continually read God's words about me in scripture, a new self-portrait was painted in my mind. Yes, I am fearfully and wonderfully made! Yes, I am a royal priesthood and a holy nation! Yes, I can do all things through Christ that strengthens me! Yes, I can be a reconciler and a "Restorer of the Streets to Dwell in" (Isaiah 58) for my family, community and nation.

I began to see and believe how God had equipped me for his assignments for my life to make a tangible spiritual difference in this world. Like an atomic bomb, God's truth of my real identity in Him blew Satan's lies to smithereens. God created me as a phenomenal human being – filled with talents, gifts and abilities – at the moment of my conception. My birth and life was divinely intentionally purposeful – not a mistake!

Once realized, received and believed, this truth ultimately allowed me to live and function in divine purpose. Living in Queenship, not victimhood, became my new normal. As I believed, and allowed God in, I excelled and flourished, even in failure and opposition, despite my beginnings (and middle), as you will read.

The same God who did this – and is doing this – for me can and will do this for you – but only if you let Him in. God is waiting for your invitation to let Him in and allow His transformation of your "self" to

authenticity and your "new normal." You, too, are in the world "for such a time as this!" Receive it. Believe it. It is true.

Incest Pandemic Survivor

Incest - The Dark Secret - Hush...

"SHHHHHHHH!"
"You better not tell *anyone* – OR ELSE!"
the 6-foot giant man said.

i'm a helpless child
orphaned then adopted

"Come here sweet child"

Uncle, why are you touching me…there?

Does anyone see?

Does anyone hear?

Does anyone care?

You're crushing my innocence
i can't stop you.
i'm frozen, scared and paralyzed with fear
When,
"You better not tell anyone"
echoes in my 8-year-old tiny ears.

My screams are choked by your nasty tongue
and fear;
What are these sensations?
I feel guilty, dirty – like *I* did something wrong.
My screams are swallowed
No one hears,

Inside this dark, forbidden basement
No one knows.
so *it* continues…
i'm filled with fright
when i visit during the day or night.

~~~~~~~~~

The child of incest suffers… alone.

I'll bury my cry deep inside;
So deep that I'll never
remember,
I'll force myself to forget.
I'll bury the violation, victimization and my helpless
unheard cries,
Deep, so deep inside….
Until one day… decades away….
When violation matures into
volcanic, internal rage
that later destroys self,
the self that let itself
be violated.

Self-destruction comes in many forms:
drug abuse to ease the pain,
choosing the abuser in each relationship the same,
domestic violence, mental and
emotional abuse become the order of the day.

Anger and rage reversed on self – by self
Because someone has to pay
Someone is to blame
sadistic behavior is the remedy
Self-mutilation hoping to relieve the pain
alcohol – to remove the shame, guilt stain –
overeating to feel good again,

lover after lover – never-learned-how-to-say "no"
paralyzed again and again,
learned about sex from childhood incest.

The cruel world says,
"The victim is to blame!"
the adult child believes the same.
"So keep hurting yourself"
"You're worthless"
Yells the voice inside your head.

but

One day **Jesus** reached down
and picked up the damaged child inside.
Held her,
Loved her,
Wiped the tears from her eyes,
and her heart…
Christ's love expressed by the shedding of His blood
for all sexual abuse,
for *yours* too,
Jesus Heard my screams,
took the sting and shame of incest away…

Only Christ can take the violation
of incest and rape away,
And replace it with
"I love you!"
"You are the apple of my eye!"
"You are valuable, full of worth that's why I died;"
"You are fearfully and wonderfully made!"
"Now share my love with others!"
"You are set free from abuse today!"

"You *are* set free from **all** abuse today!"

I wish I could say that when the molestation ended when I was 11 years old, (it had lasted approximately 4 years) I was healed, but that was not the case. Even after I accepted Christ at the age of 11, there were still deep, deep scars and fresh wounds from that childhood experience that would take decades of God's grace to heal, restore, reconcile and repair.

I buried this "dark secret" deep, deep inside. But it came out in other ways. When it came to men touching me and making advances, "No" got stuck in my throat. Unfortunately, my fear and unleashed-too-soon sexuality made me a prime target for teenage boys and young men. Even in the church, a few took advantage of my vulnerability, thereby adding additional guilt and shame to my already shameful self – the by-product of child molestation.

However, there was one young man who never tried to take advantage of me in any way (he was a little bit of a nerd himself). I eventually chose him to be my first child's godfather. He and his wife celebrated my daughter's birth, childhood, adolescent and adult life. Little did I know that decades later, my daughter's godfather would become the Senior Pastor and Bishop of my church.

By God's grace, despite the trauma of my experiences, I survived and received continual healing from the Lord – over time. Jesus had given me his presence that went deep into the wound of my childhood trauma – from abandonment as an infant and child molestation and abuse, which led to extreme fear of rejection and separation issues. But because of God's love, the precious Blood of Jesus, and the priceless scriptures in the bible, plus prayers – my prayers as a child and teenager – God began and continued the healing process of restoring my soul, mind and emotions. There is one theme in my life. No matter what happens, God has been there and will continue to be there every step of the way. I have survived.

Domestic Violence...The Cycle Continues...

"I'm sorry, it will never happen again."
"I love you."
That's what my baby's daddy said.
While in the ambulance, those words swirled around my head.
Eight months pregnant beaten up from sunrise to night,
kicked me where his baby lied inside,
All because of jealous rage.
When will my life turn the page?
I love him.
He said he loved me.
But why should love to hurt?
Who can I talk to?
I'm so ashamed,
Afraid to press charges,
Scared he'll come back and beat me again.

I later took him back – to my shame.
I didn't want to raise my baby alone.
Anyway, he'll change it won't take long…
The cycle of domestic violence sometimes never ends.
Until at her funeral we say our last
Amen!

Intimate Partner Violence Pandemic Survivor

Living Hell

I was raised in a clean, abundant, classy, middle class, family oriented and an ultimately Christian home (I was saved before my parents), where a strong work ethic and values were important. In the cooperative community where I lived, the grounds and buildings were kept immaculate. Security guards patrolled the grounds and secured the beautiful lush green landscape, filled with maple and wild berry trees, and trees that boasted of white/pink apple blossoms in the spring.

In the winter, three majestic evergreens raised their brown barked boughs to the sun and the evening moon. These majestic evergreens were decorated with lights and a Menorah during the Christmas Season. But one fateful day in 1979, at the age of 19, I left my home, where I was loved and nurtured and all of my beautiful life – on the arm of my "Man." As I went from the sublime to the ridiculous, he escorted me to his home, or should I say, his mother's apartment in a project located in the center of hell.

Before we left, he paused at the elevator on my floor, bent his head, shoulders and arms downward in exasperated fear and sighed; "Now I have to take care of you." I followed him into his provision for my life, a two-bedroom apartment in the project on 115th Street, East Harlem. His room was shared with his younger brothers, an 11-year-old on the top bunk and an overweight 8-year-old who peed on the bottom bunk every night.

The frequent smell of urine and drab dreary look of the roach-infested room was my "honeymoon suite," where my boyfriend and I slept in a twin size bed. I cried in pain and agony one night because the bathroom was so filled with spider webs and roaches, I could not take

a bath, only a shower, and my very special and precious private place was burning and could find no relief.

Finally, his mother said, "Girl wash out the tub." She must have seen the petrified look on my face, but I took the rag and scrubbed and scrubbed until every trace of grime, dirt and neglect had been washed away. I will never forget the soothing warm water that brought healing to my worn body and torn soul.

He and I had little in common. We met on a temporary job at Bank Street College. I thought he was a working man; how naïve I was. We did have some shared interests, two detrimental habits: smoking weed, in those days we called it "herb" (a colloquial term for marijuana) and drinking beer like it was soda, even Old English, which was really nasty. I still remember the "gasoline" taste. Believe it or not, I felt like I was living. I felt claimed by this man who loved me and showered me with attention. But the man who "took care of me" could not even take care of himself. He quickly stopped getting temporary assignments, because he was unqualified and uneducated, and soon resumed his role as a black man on welfare – hustling.

At one point I was working two jobs: at Alexander's, in the gourmet department and at Macy's as a buyer's clerical. He continued to collect welfare, and worked odd jobs with his motley crew, as I was getting used to my new lifestyle and becoming a product of my new environment of oppression, poverty and hopelessness.

His mother survived on credit from the grocery store and food stamps, so once a month the freezer and refrigerator were full, but at month's end, they were completely empty. Then she survived on credit and the generosity of her best friend.

When I went upstairs to his mother's best friend's apartment it was amazing – it was a different world. She had a beautiful home, clean, full of warmth, appliances and good furniture. It was like the Honeymooners, Ralph living in scarcity in a drab home, while Norton lived in abundance, bright, fresh and crisp. One day, the second day,

she called me upstairs and pleaded with me to go back to my mother, to go back to my home, because this place, especially downstairs, was no place for me. But me and my arrogant, foolish teenage pride, "I'm-a-woman-now, out-from-under-my-mother's-iron fist, endless rules and unfair oppression self," refused to go home.

My life had become a mess, to say the least, but believe it or not, I was enjoying myself living the project life with my new friends – his friends and family. I was isolated from my family and most of my friends, especially those in church that I grew up with, as well as the wonderful life I once knew, because I was "in love."

Wow, I look back at those times, it was amazing I survived that season of my life. Thank God to the utmost, Jesus saves and His Grace is sufficient! For one day the fun stopped and I knew I had made a terrible mistake. Late in the night, while everyone was asleep, I went into the living room and I cried my eyes out to God in quiet desperation. Jesus' presence was felt in the room and inside me that night to hold my wounded soul and shattered life and heart. God was with me – even in hell on earth.

But still, I stayed. I was hooked on "sex, drugs and rock & roll" in the projects. I was no longer a nerd who had to be upstairs at 11p.m., who wore funny shoes and clothes, who couldn't dance, curse, only went to church, and was too smart for the rest of her peers – I was finally "down" and became a good dancer – eventually a "house music" regular. Even my friends said I surpassed them. No longer was I ostracized like I had been for my entire childhood and most of my teenage years in my neighborhood. I was a woman living with a man and I was "cool." I didn't realize my true identity was lost. I traded my authenticity, my true self, for a mask of popularity, compromise and distortion.

Soon my "man" found an apartment for us. It was a splendid one-bedroom apartment in one of the notorious welfare tenements on 118th Street and Pleasant Avenue, the Italian section of Harlem. Up

until that point I never knew that there was an "Italian" section of Harlem, only Blacks and Puerto Ricans (they were not called Hispanics yet, neither were Blacks called "African Americans.")

We walked upstairs to our suite on the fourth floor, where we saw garbage in the hallway by the steps on every high floor. In our apartment, the tub was in the kitchen and was covered with a lid that doubled as counter space. The bathroom was the size of a broom closet and had a toilet and sink. We had no heat in the winter and we froze. We were forced to use the pilot lights from the stove and the oven because the pipes had no heat. We slept on a mattress that he found in the street. Thank God my mother taught me about sheets and mattress covers. By the grace of God, we survived. Still I did not go home. Little did I know, the fun was about to begin.

My boyfriend remained on welfare, while I was trying to make something out of my life. I followed a lead to an organization called, "Jobs for Youth." I registered at 19 ½ and began the CEDA program, where I was paid a stipend. I learned how to type and was promised job placement once I completed the program. They also offered GED preparation.

Since I already had my High School Regents Diploma from Bronx High School of Science, I tutored many of the young ladies – my peers. Many of them shared the same lifestyle that had become my "norm." During one occasion, my lovely 23-year-old "man" demanded sex from me, but I said "No," because I was so sore. He was rather well endowed and was destroying my tender, 19-year-old insides. But he would not take "no" for an answer.

One morning, I was on my way to the program, we had to be on time, and I had seven blocks to walk to the bus. He refused to stop harassing me and walked, or should I say followed me to the bus, making his demands in a threatening tone. When I attempted to climb the steps of the bus he dragged me into the street, pushed me around,

and held my arm like a child and took me back home. That was my introduction into domestic violence.

Unfortunately, that was not the last occurrence. We always fought for the same reason – sex. We even fought after we broke up. I was so hooked I still kept coming to the house to try to get him back. Co-dependency coupled with the cycle of domestic violence is a recipe for destruction and disaster. We finally broke up when he came to my job and stole my bag from under me because he wanted to buy a car with all of the money I earned. In tears, with my "tail between my legs" I shamefully returned home, but it was never the same.

There was such a distance between me and my parents, especially with my mother. My father was hurt and disappointed, but my mother, I can't explain it – there was a wall of hurt and anger at me that took decades to come down. I felt like I was a bad little girl that desperately wanted her mother's approval and forgiveness. But my parents did take me in, I was their daughter and they loved me – even though they were extremely hurt and frustrated with what their daughter and her life had become.

After two weeks, totally oblivious to reality, driven by emptiness and a deep heart hunger, I went back to make amends and reunite with my abuser. When I put my key into the door a 16-year-old teenager was in my apartment – with my man. I was replaced. He snatched the keys from me and told me to go, then slammed the door in my face. I was devastated and lost.

Months later I returned to him again, this time he was living with a woman who was a crack addict, back in his mother's apartment. When I knocked on the door, he came out into the staircase with me and we physically fought again. This time, I was fighting just as hard as he was. I wanted him so badly that even an altercation was welcomed contact (warped, isn't it?). Eventually, he and the crack addict had a child together, his first. Years later, I saw him with his little girl; she was about three years old (he had custody). He was using her to help

him beg for money on the train with a sob story. The next time I saw him, about a year later, he was a representative for Coalition for the Homeless soliciting funds, again, on the train. I never saw him again. I survived. I moved ahead and never looked back.

Domestic Violence – Part 11

I met him at the Paradise Garage in Tribeca. He was mesmerizingly "fine" – an Adonis -with his beautiful Indian influenced caramel chocolate toned skin and perfectly hanging – not dripping-looking-like-natural-hair Jeri Curls, six foot tall "brother" who simply said, "Can you pass me a napkin? I'll give you a dance." One year and three months later, when "Ahhhhhh" became "Waaaaaah!" our beautiful baby daughter, Dejshona, (he named her) was born in 1983. I was 23 years old.

Unfortunately, my pregnancy was not without incident. When I was eight months pregnant, he flew into a jealous rage and kicked and beat me for an entire day, until a neighbor called the police. I let him leave without pressing charges. I did not understand the system; I was deathly scared of him and I didn't want him to hear my request to the police.

After he left, I asked if I could press charges. The policeman told me it was too late. Thank God, when I arrived at the hospital my fetus was fine, but I was black and blue in my eyes, body and soul.

Later that week, I went to the funeral of a dear mother of the church, Sister Kelly, with sunglasses on (It was February). When two brothers (actual brothers), who loved me like a sister, saw my face they were ready to put whoever did this to me "lights out." My pastor was so hurt he could barely look at me. But in shame I told them it was alright, that he was gone.

Eventually, my daughter's father returned and we got back together. During my pregnancy was not the first time he had hit me... The first time he hit me was in the head with a shoe for wanting to go

to his sister's wedding – they were estranged. My mother stopped my uncle and family from "taking matters into their own hands" because she regrettably told me that if they helped me and I went back to him, they would never help me again. She never wanted that to happen.

No one understood the dynamics of rage, tremendous fear and intimidation, physical and sexual assault and the making up period only to be repeated again and again and again. I was helplessly trapped in the cycle of domestic violence, fueled by deep insecurity rooted in abandonment, rejection, low self-worth, "identity" crisis and severe co-dependency (which I didn't understand until almost three decades later.), drugs and rock and roll.

Tragically, this was not the first or last beating I would endure. Interestingly enough, after my daughter was born, he came up to the altar and accepted Christ; he even went to new convert's class – but he did not change. My mentor warned me that just because he went up to the altar it didn't mean he had changed. She advised me to stay away from him and separate. Unfortunately, I was too addicted to him and was raising a baby – his baby – so we continued to live together.

When my daughter was five months old and I stopped breastfeeding, I could no longer stand welfare and began looking for work. I found a great job at Knoll International in Soho. My mother babysat and eventually secured a Provide-a-Mother – in house certified babysitter with a regulated home. Since my mother was on the Board of Directors of the Soundview Day Care Center who employed my caregiver, she was able to frequently monitor the home where my daughter was being cared for while I was at work.

Since I lived across town, it became difficult to get across the Bronx by bus and then back to the west side to take the train to Soho. So we (or rather she) decided that it would be best for my daughter to stay with her during the week and I would get her on the weekends. Surprisingly, whenever Dejshona was around, her father did not lay a hand on me, only when she was gone.

One day when were taking a shower together he tried to wash my back and I cringed. He looked at me and said, "You don't love me anymore, do you?" I remained silent, finished washing and walked out of the tub. In my heart, I realized that I had fallen out of love with him. I was moving on with my life but he was standing still.

During those times, I still went out when I could, since my mother had my daughter that usually meant during the week. On Tuesdays after work, I would go with my girlfriend to this punk, deep house, underground club called Dancenteria. But this particular Tuesday I was feeling under the weather and decided to go home straight after work. When I got there and put the key in the door, the chain lock was on. A woman removed the chain lock and opened the door, it was my "baby's daddy's" other woman, and I noticed she was about 7 or 8 months pregnant with his baby.

Consequently, my daughter has a wonderful brother about six months younger than her, who is a responsible and wonderful husband and father. My daughter met her brother decades later, as an adult. He also has accepted Christ into his heart and life.

Getting back to the incident when I walked into the house I flipped. He told her to leave, and we had a knock-them-down-drag-out brawl. Then, a thought came to my mind that this is not getting me anywhere, and I stopped throwing punches. Surprisingly, he was more defending himself than hitting me, so when I stopped, he stopped.

I went into the bathroom, washed my face, fixed my hair and put on make-up. I came out of the bathroom and told him, "Let's go for a walk." He felt and looked so guilty that he would do anything I would say to try to make up. I had a plan that was beginning to play out in my mind as we walked each step towards a friend's mother-in-law's home.

Once I arrived, I introduced them. She asked him to sit down in the living room. After he sat down, I whispered to her, "Meet me in the kitchen." I briefly told her that I was going to call the police and would she keep him occupied in the living room. I called the police to report

the domestic violence incident and told them that I wanted him out of my house because I feared for my life.

When they arrived, we both went outside, escorted by the police. They asked him if he lived there. He said yes. The police then asked if his clothes were there, to which he responded yes. The police then released him and he left. The police then informed me that because he lived there and his clothes and belongings were there that by law, they could not remove him from my home. (This was in 1983.) But they told me that they would take me wherever I wanted to go. They escorted me back to my apartment, and I took a few clothes and left to return to my parents' home.

I left him in the apartment but I took my life with me. By the Grace of God, His mercy and His loving compassion I found a new, bigger, one-bedroom apartment in a private house in less than a week. I called my former landlord and told him I was moving immediately. Then, I called Con-Edison to turn off the electricity and gas. I returned to the apartment with a mover and my parents for protection and to assist me.

On the way down on the elevator, I heard my father yell, "He's going down the steps." When I got to the first floor, I took off my shoe and when the door opened, he was standing there. I stood up to him, for the first time. I looked him dead in the eye and I told him if he touched me, I would hit him in his face with my heel. He stepped aside and let me leave. I moved out of my own apartment and left him there. I finally escaped the throngs of domestic abuse and violence – I was free. Praise God I came out alive – I survived.

We were never together as a couple again. The only contact we had was concerning our daughter. Despite what happened, as long as he respected our daughter and me, I kept the door of communication open between him and my child. I never tried to turn my daughter against her father, I let her decide if she wanted contact with him or not.

They had a sporadic relationship. In his own way, he loved her. She was the best creation in his life (besides his son) and he knew it and expressed it the best way he was able. Unfortunately, he had a history of violence spurred on by alcoholism and was incarcerated several times. However, to my knowledge he managed to not return to prison and he maintained his own apartment, while still dealing with demons of his past and issues of the present.

He had an abusive and troubled past (he was a runaway at 16). His unreconciled issue was buried into rage with other issues. I prayed and interceded for him throughout the years. My prayer was that God forgave him, redeemed him, saved his soul and his life – and that through God's love, he was able to forgive himself. But I moved on.

Closure...

On December 2, 2019, at the wake of the coronavirus global pandemic, he died in a men's shelter in New York City. No one knew of his death until almost a month later. My daughter called me with the news on New Year's Eve. I was stunned!

Even though he was no longer a part of my life, I had since forgiven him and on occasion prayed for him. He had become a part of my daughter's life in seasons and we made our peace. He even told me when my twins were born, "Elle, I accept your twins." Not that I needed his approval or acceptance, but he felt he needed to say that. He battled with anger and alcohol. His death-day was also his birthday. He died at 60 years old.

Though one chapter was completely closed, there was a lingering page not stamped with "the end." My daughter had a younger brother. At a beautiful memorial service hosted by my daughter's aunt, we all celebrated their father's memory and life and released floating white balloon-like lanterns to the heavens and said good-bye.

My daughter, his first child, sang with a sweet, beautiful angelic voice, "Savior, Savior hear my humble cry, while on others thou art

calling, do not pass me by." The love she had for God and her father filled the room and touched every heart, as members of her father's family and myself shed tears of loss and admiration for his "baby girl."

My daughter's brother was one of the most amazing young men, and the two of them were two peas in a pod. They met for the first time about 12 years before that memorial, and she became an instant part of his family. He had a wife and two lovely children. But I was confronted with the sordid realty of how he became my daughter's brother. I was faced with the reality that his mother and I shared the same living room, space and "baby's daddy."

When a box of pictures of my daughter's father was passed around, I saw the picture of him and her looking amorous like Ashford and Simpson, as she stood in front of him and leaned back on his supportive body. They had the most serious look of love, as if they were made for eternity, never to be separated, not even by pregnant me. It crushed my soul all over again, after 40 years.

All of the horrible memories of deception, and up in your face infidelity were raw – not as painful, but still recognizable. A relative asked me, "Scared you might fight her?" I looked at him almost like he was crazy and reassured him that was not going to happen. But maybe he saw something in my eyes, face or gestures. Or maybe he too remembered the truth, because he was there, his brothers were there, the whole family knew about their past and present relationship.

Everyone but me knew, until it was smashed in my face and resulted in my retaliation in kind – that sparked a jealous rage in him – that ended with me in the Jacobi Hospital Emergency Room at 8 months pregnant after being beaten up throughout the day. Abandoned by my best friend and neighbor, when I didn't press charges, because I did not understand the system and was fearful of his retaliation.

At first, I tried to ignore the "elephant in the room" and not talk about or confront what happened over 4 decades ago. But I realized that without honest conversation, a crack in the door of pain would still be

open, fertilizing and resurrecting a dead root, left to grow with each moment we spent in the same space.

So, when all the family had gone outside to release the lanterns representing his spirit ascending, I finally cracked the ice. We both shared our truths and clarified 40 years of air. We both left free and unencumbered by our past; we both asked for forgiveness and received forgiveness. In his death, the memories and power of pain died too. What emerged were resurrected lives as we enjoyed each other's family, our children – brother and sister, not half, but whole.

As I saw all of the members from her father's family, I felt the love, acceptance, fun and joy I always remembered. I always loved my daughter's father's big family of 10 children – since I was an only child. Where there was once excruciating pain there was now the joy of surviving this pandemic of domestic violence and betrayal, using the vaccination of forgiveness, God's healing love and closing this door. I knew it was all over and I was about to step into a new threshold of peace, joy and love – God's future for me.

His untimely death led to unexpected closure. This event permanently closed the chapter of pain, domestic violence, trauma and abuse associated with that early season of my life that thrust me into motherhood. I was completely able to turn the last page of the chapter in joy, restoration and peace. The same God who provided healing and closure for me – is ready, willing and able to heal and restore joy for you,

Isaiah 51:3 (KJV)

For the LORD shall comfort Zion: he will comfort all her waste places; and he will make her wilderness like Eden, and her desert like the garden of the LORD; joy and gladness shall be found therein, thanksgiving, and the voice of melody.

Single Parenthood Pandemic Survivor

Shooting the "J"

Conflict

I want to scream inside.
Pastor, What do you do?
When there's no male presence in your home,
To provide the male example and
guidance that this sermon prescribes.

What happens to my children –
do their hopes and dreams die?
Help, Help, Help I'm a single mother drowning!
Don't you see me?
I'm bleeding!
Don't you care?
I'm about to flat line…
But nobody knows, nobody sees
Because my bleeding is inside.

I'm lonely, abused, exhausted,
depressed and at times confused;
I can't block out life,
The x-factor has caused so much strife;
The x-factor has killed and crushed my spirit,
Who will life me up?

Who will lift up my children and me?
Jesus…I'm a woman infirmed
Like the woman in the parable;
I can't help myself, by myself;
I can't straighten up my back

I'm too bent over;
I can't even life my head;
My faith is not enough to life me up – it's so faint…

What do you do when the faith won't come?
When I'm too bent over,
Due to decades of infirmity,
Like the woman in the parable;
18 years of infirmity.
I can't look up;
I can't believe;
What do I do?
I'm crying on my bent, broken, knees…
Jesus, saints, church, please help me!
So I can look into the face of Jesus;
So I can believe too;
I have a speck of faith – but I still need your help,
Don't leave me alone;
I'm bleeding to death from the fiery darts;
I look like Jesus did in the Passion of the,
Christ…On the inside.

Church you are my last stop.
My last hope
Don't leave it up to me to pull myself up by my own
"Bootstraps"
I'm rejected, abandoned, forlorn, thrown away, and mixed up;
Strength to pull myself up is all gone…

Church, Pastors, Counselors, Saints and Family
When a person is bleeding
First you have to stop the bleeding;
First you have to perform CPR,
Before healing and recovery can begin.

Church, Pastors, Jesus…someone!
Stop my bleeding!
Stop the crushing of my soul and
Then I can, I will believe, have faith and fight!

I'm screaming inside because of the pain,
Does anybody hear me? See me?
Pastor, Elder, Minister, Mother, Father, Friend

Do you hear my scream?

He asked you,
Can't Jesus show you my pain?
It's just me and Jesus,
Just the same.

Yes you, who are spiritual,
To loose me of my grace clothes
And set me free!
Graves clothes of abuse self-hatred, self-destruction, slander,
Dishonor…pain;
I need more than what you are giving,
I need your help, just the same,
Life up your head,
Point me to Jesus,
Lift up my arms,
Help me life them
So I can worship God too!

I need help!
I can't loose myself!
Do you hear me?
Look at the infirmed woman in the parable,
She couldn't loose herself.

Church, please, be moved with compassion
Not moved with blame…

RESOLUTION

Well if no one is around,
Will I and my children die?
My spirit deep inside faintly yells,
No, No, No!

I will get up off the ground;
I'm barely able to encourage myself,
But in pain, through pain I purpose to open my mouth
I cry, "I worship you, Lord!'
I finally say;
I will be renewed, restored and freed!
I say it, even if I don't feel it,
Through God's grace and strength
The Blood of Jesus presides;
By His Love, His Word, His Command
I will renew my walk,
I will get up and walk by faith,
Not by sight!
So get up – Myself
Myself, get up and walk
Just walk by faith;
Jesus has the master plan;
Just keep hold of His hand;
Your destiny is to be loosed not bound;
Your destiny is to get up;
Stop asking why,
Your destiny is to live…not die!

Infirmed Woman, mother, man or child Jesus says,

Thou Art Loosed!
In the Name of Jesus

Get Up!!!

Get Up!!

Get Up!

The Beginning.

El Roi

GOD Sees Me

Being a single parent raising twin boys-to-men and a precious daughter was not a walk-in-the park. But God understood my concerns. In the Bible, I saw myself. That is why the story in Genesis (chapters 16 and 21) about Hagar is so precious to me. First, as a servant and concubine Hagar was under the thumb of those who had control of her destiny. Then she ran away from the contentions and disdain of a woman, whose idea it was to sleep with her husband to have a child, who then kicked her out. On the run, Hagar was met by an angel who said to her in the desert, "What are you doing here?" "Return, your provisions are not here in the desert [of rejection] but in the house of your mistress." Haggar then responded, "and she called the name of the Lord that spake unto her, Thou God seest me." (Genesis 16:13) In other words, she looked up to God, and said, "God, You See Me" – in the Hebrew "El Roi".

There have been many times as a single parent that I felt totally alone raising my children, inept, ill equipped, not enough money, shelter, food, provisions and hope. I remember the time I ran out of money on public assistance and I only had one pamper left for my twins. I had to decide which twin would stay in a wet, soiled diaper risking sever diaper rash, and which infant would be changed and relieved. On the way home I broke down and cried.

NO mother should have to make that choice. Unfortunately, this can happen when a woman raises her children without the support and caring of their father. However, before I go further. There are many single mothers and fathers who have managed to keep a household and children going, with necessary and abundant provisions. We salute you!

However, for many that is not their experience. It can be an overwhelming struggle. Especially the feeling of isolation and uncertainty – like this pandemic. Tragically and historically in America, statistics for decades (and probably centuries) showed that the lowest demographic on the economic scale, below the poverty line, are women and children. I was employed all my life (even as a teen), until I was eight months pregnant with twins. The real estate law firm I worked for lease was not renewed and subsequently, relocated out of New York City.

Not uncommonly, at 29, I did not have sufficient savings, unemployment ran out and we eventually needed welfare to survive. But public assistance was never enough, kept us in bondage and beholden to a racist welfare system for sustenance. But thank God it did not last forever and God kept us – even in dire moments. Finally, the way off welfare for me and my children was through education – from victim to victor in the middle!

Faithfully, God saw me and my children – El Roi. Our family survived, learned to thrive during this season. I earned two degrees while on public assistance for five years, my AAS in Paralegal Studies, six scholarships, fellowships, awards, honors and earned a Bachelor of Arts in Political Science, Cum Laude. In each scholarship essay, I included how I maintained academic excellence despite the horrendous obstacles in my life. I had the opportunity while on welfare, attending Bronx Community College to speak in Harlem to formerly homeless women.

The crux of my message was that homelessness, public assistance or whatever the dilemma you face with your children – there is life beyond any horrific experiences. The same way I went to school on welfare, found childcare on welfare, completed an AAS in Paralegal studies with honors on welfare, excelled and made a life for me and my

children, (and eventually completed my Bachelor of Arts in Political Science) – each person that reads this book can as well! Eventually, I was inducted as the Phi Theta Kappa President as a single parent on welfare with a high GPA. I had the honor and privilege to induct four students with 4.0 GPA's from Sing Sing Correctional Facility into the honor society Phi Theta Kappa. I was humbled as I saw these men against all odds, go to school, apply themselves and come out academically victorious. It gave me even more determination to continue on my path of academic excellence and bring as many people as I could along with me.

Throughout my twin pregnancy I was frequently hospitalized and experienced hardships. Continually, God used every situation to show me that He would never abandon me or my three children. God proved He could provide for us throughout any ordeal and the rest of our lives. For example, I remember when I was seven months pregnant with my twins. Unfortunately, the law firm I worked for, lost their lease and relocated out of New York City during my last trimester. They placed me on unemployment and it was soon to run out. I spent my last few insufficient dollars on food. At the register when I was leaving, I looked down. There was a $20.00 bill. My spirits immediately lifted when I thought, "This is a sign that God sees me, knows what's going on and will provide for me. I don't have to worry – God's got me!" So, just like Hagar, at a crucial moment I experienced "El Roi" – God saw me.

Poverty Pandemic Survivor via Academic Excellence!

From Welfare Role to Honor Role

Another major reason I wrote this book is to share my life's journey with the millions of mothers and children who have struggled to survive and thrive like I have.

When I found out I was pregnant with twins six years after my daughter was born, a chill of panic overtook me. On that October day in 1989, I screamed to God and cried so loud my neighbor came downstairs banged on the door and said, "Who is here beating you?" I said "No one." It took a while to convince him that I was ok. However, I was not ok. I cried to God that I could not take care of these babies alone as a single parent. What am I going to do? I can't do this God!

As time went on God's response was, "I never intended for you to raise them alone, without me." God was true to his word and helped me through every dark and bright moment as a single parent of twin boys.

Through God's grace, determination and creativity I learned to survive during five years of receiving public assistance while turning lemons into lemonade. During my seventh month of pregnancy with my twins, my employer informed me that they would be relocating to Lake Success, NY because their lease was not renewed. They graciously offered me unemployment, since I used up my maternity leave due to severe problems during my pregnancy that had required numerous hospitalizations and bed rest.

Unfortunately, my twin's father was unemployed, hustled and ultimately out of our lives, (he returned to a former relationship) so I struggled with the reality that I would be raising my infants on

unemployment until it ran out. I hoped I would find a babysitter and a new job.

I endured a rough pregnancy, and when my children were born, it took over six months before I found childcare for my twins. I had to go through the Agency For Child Development, via the New York Foundling Crisis Nursery, and was given childcare as a result of their prevention program. I had used their services as a result of overwhelming physical, mental and emotional stress of raising twin colicky babies and high-energy toddlers alone, coupled with sleep deprivation and financial need.

The Crisis Nursery kept my infants in their state-of-the-art facility for two to three days while I handled my affairs, appointments and got a well needed break and some sleep before I broke down. A good friend told me that her cousin had a nervous breakdown from caring for twins alone. I did not want that to happen to me, so I sought help. I also found another Crisis Nursery in the Bronx, the Prospect Inn. Both provided emergency assistance and I will never regret seeking help.

There is no shame in reaching out for help when you need it, especially when it comes to raising children. Many of the mothers who have unintentionally or intentionally harmed or killed their children felt trapped, with no help or place to go. This is where the church can help by reaching out to single parents, sometimes watching their children or intervening in other positive ways. We all need each other; nobody is immune to stress.

My unemployment eventually ran out and I was forced to go on dreaded public assistance (welfare) in order to survive and take care of my three children. During those times (and before) my mother raised and housed my daughter and helped me so I could use my limited resources for my sons and my survival.

Being on welfare was one of the most dehumanizing experiences in my life. The system drains you of your time, dignity and

sometimes your hope. But I stuck it out because I had children to take care of with no support from their fathers. Through welfare I was able to shelter, feed and clothe them, take care of their medical needs, go to school to improve our situation, and get off welfare.

Thank God my landlord (a relative) was willing to work with me, since I was allotted less than $400 a month for rent. During this time I was living in a basement studio apartment with my twins sons and my daughter on the weekends – but we survived (termites and all). In the winter it was so cold that the water pipes froze. I had to get water from a taxi depot across a busy street to have water to flush the toilet and boil for drinking and cooking.

As I look back it was only the grace of God that kept me alive, even when I felt like I was in despair and freezing. One day I was so cold I threw a fit, upturned the kitchen table and cried uncontrollably as I suffered with my children in the cold. I could not believe that I was living in these conditions and I had no other place to live that I could afford.

However, no matter the crisis, whenever I cried out to God, He heard my cry. As a single parent I quickly learned the value of prayer. My "prayer closet" was the bathroom. (The twins had my bedroom, I slept in the living room.) So, with the door closed I found safety, sanity and "personal space." I quickly learned that prayer was the most valuable weapon in my single parent arsenal. I developed a daily quiet time of conversation with God – prayer, learning about God and his promises for me in the Bible and I experienced His presence through the Holy Spirit. I was safe and secure in that special, sacred space. As I made room for God in my life, especially during storms, He was always there. That is how I survived the numerous single parent storms, crisis, sometimes loneliness and the mundane of *"motherhood"* routines.

Additionally, at night as my children grew into adolescence, I would anoint them with oil as they sleep and prayed over them. I knew

that these prayers followed them, kept them safe, kept them alive – especially as Black sons. We also had a family time of prayer, sharing and Bible reading through adolescence. I remember one evening, we marched and danced around the coffee table joyously singing a song we learned during a church trip to Oregon (another amazing experience!) We sang and shouted, "I went to the enemy's camp and I took back what he stole from me, took back what he stole from me, took back what he stole from me. I went to the enemy's camp and I took back what he stole from me. He's under my feet, He's under my feet, satan is under my feeeeeet!" It was a blast and a family memory that I will never forget. Single parent families do not have to function in dysfunction, but in love and joy – with "Christ" in the middle. Dear, wonderful, phenomenal single parent take hope. You are not alone…

Victory Along the Way…

By the time my twins were a year old, I had not found a job and had to make an important decision. Do I want to continue to look for a job as a legal secretary/administrative assistant, or do I want to finish college and gain skills for a viable career utilizing my God given gifts, talents and abilities? My former employer had given me unemployment since the job relocated – but it had run out. It was a risk, but I decided to take the hard road, sacrifice financially, and go on welfare while pursuing a college degree.

So, one summer day in 1991, I took my year-old twin infants in their double McClaren stroller on the Bronx Express Bus to Hunter College in Manhattan. This began my educational journey, which lasted 14 years, culminating in three degrees and 30 postgraduate credits – of which I only paid for 51 undergraduate credits. Half of my BA, 100% of my MSED and 30 credits above my masters were financed through scholarships, fellowships, grants and awards. All of my tuition was paid!

God is amazingly good, despite the hardships I faced that made me stronger, wiser and resilient. God was with me through my tears,

through my fears. God never left me or abandoned me even though the men in my life and sometimes others did. Many times I felt alone and cried to God that I could not do this by myself, and His presence would fill my heart and calm my fears.

Guess what, God never intended for me to do this alone, but to rely on Him. I learned this through trial by fire. Sometimes the consequences of our choices result in situations that cause us to totally rely on God – or it is over. Had I not gone through so many horrific experiences, I would not have known that God was able to hold and carry me when life became overwhelming and the problems were bigger than me. But I learned that no problem is bigger than God. As Apostle Mark Excel stated frequently, "We serve a big, big God!"

Unfortunately, due to the policies of public assistance at that time I could only attend a community college or vocational program, although I had obtained 51 undergraduate credits at Hunter College in New York City. Before I got my transcript, I owed financial aid from 18 years prior when I dropped out of college and moved out of my parents' home at 19 years old.

My wise, resourceful and financially smart mother had savings bonds for me, which she had accumulated since my birth and held for me until I was an adult. She did not tell me anything about the savings bonds until that time. This was another example of God's provision for his will in my life.

With the savings bonds, I had enough funds to cover the entire tuition in default and thereby obtain my transcript needed to enroll in Bronx Community College (BCC). BCC had their own day care program and I found a wonderful provider-mother in a new private house to care for my sons across the street from BCC.

Again, God came through for my family and me in a spectacular way. I graduated Bronx Community College with an AAS in Paralegal/Lay Advocacy and earned a 3.95 GPA. This high GPA allowed me to receive numerous scholarships, as I utilized the

hardships and obstacles as a single parent – my story – as I wrote essay after essay for each scholarship.

These scholarships enabled me to complete Hunter College without paying one penny for tuition – despite lack of financial assistance from welfare – to obtain a degree from any four-year college. One scholarship, the Bell Zeller Scholarship, paid for my entire tuition for as long as it took for me to complete my undergraduate studies at Hunter, as long as I maintained a 3.0 GPA. Once again, God's grace allowed me to go from victim to victor despite governmental politics and policies.

As an added bonus, my internship in the Hunter Public Service Scholars Program was with HRA, Human Resources Administration (welfare) in the Data Analysis Department. My project was to critique and analyze the public assistance 45-day application process for the New York City Way initiative and make suggestions for improvement. Amazingly, God enabled me to critique and analyze the very agency that tried to deny me an undergraduate degree from a four-year educational institution.

Ultimately, I graduated Hunter College, which I began 18 years prior, at the age of 36 years old. I am a living testimony that you are never too old, or in too dire a circumstance to obtain a college degree and fulfill a lifetime goal. Again, God moved me from being a victim and used those circumstances to make me a victor.

In other words, what the devil meant for evil God used for good. God constantly uses the stumbling blocks of life as stepping-stones to opportunities and advancement in our lives. To God be the glory great things he has done! Know that God is "no respecter of persons," what he has done for me he will do for you! Trust him and see for yourself.

Through education, I was able to move my family off welfare to financial independence and a better way of life. It is my privilege to share my story so others can be encouraged to survive, thrive, persevere and endure to reach goals, destiny and purpose fulfilled. That is the

benefit of being a born-again believer and child of God. God orders the steps of his children and leads us right into abundant blessings.

Also, as the late Bishop Emeritus Ezra N. Williams stated, "Man's extremity is God's opportunity." "For with God nothing shall be impossible." God allows us to accomplish what would be seemingly impossible by ourselves. It was by God's grace and provision through education, hope and belief implanted deep inside that I had a purpose and destiny beyond welfare and acute poverty. This prevented me from getting stuck in the vicious cycle of welfare, poverty, helplessness, hopelessness and becoming another urban single parent statistic and tragedy.

Quality, trustworthy childcare was a big issue as a single parent. Childcare was imperative in order to provide for my family and complete my education. I thank God for all the people he put in my path to help me reach my goals, especially the late Gloria Gadsden and her late son David, Marcus and Billy who watched my young sons so I could complete my undergraduate degree at Hunter.

Due to school and completing assignments, sometimes I was unable to pick up my babies until after 11p.m. Their generosity afforded me the opportunity to work, complete my education and improve the life of my children. The wonderful people who helped me also included my late parents Alphonso and Anna George, my late Aunt Lorraine and Uncle Everette Jones, Dolly Spigner, Ms. Queenie and her husband Mr. Boyce, my cousins, especially Michele Ramsey, Laura Young and the late Beverly Hazel and all the ACD and BCC provider-a-mothers for my three children, church family and friends – especially my best friend and my children's godmother Dr. Doreen Stewart and godfather Russell Harper.

Thank you for your love and support. This was a crucial element of God's grace and provision as God moved me from being a *victim* to becoming a *victor*. "To God be the glory great things he has done" for my family and me. God restored what the "locust, cankerworm,

palmerworm and caterpillar" (Joel 2:25) had eaten away from my educational life, career and self-esteem.

This was just one example of God's continual renewal and restoration from the destruction experienced in my life so that my "latter days were greater than my former." God not only restored and renewed my spiritual life (over and over) but my secular and professional life as well.

The director of human resources was one of my instructors in the Hunter College's Public Service Scholars program which included 18 free credits and an internship paying a monthly stipend (which I received while on welfare and filed taxes). She told me she would hire me as soon as I obtained my degree.

One week after receiving my BA in Political Science (Cum Laude), I was hired by Victim Services as a prevention program assistant. The rest is history. I am always awed and amazed at how God works "all things together for my good." (Romans 8:28) Keep reading – there are more miracles and restoration to come, as I moved from victim to victor.

In 2001, I applied to the New York City Teaching Fellows program (which is still in existence in the NYC Department of Education) and was accepted. Consequently, I was trained as a teacher, and given Kaplan test prep for all three New York State examinations required to become a licensed teacher in New York State financially covered by the NYC Department of Education.

I obtained a Master of Science in Education from Lehman College with a 3.75 GPA, totally funded by the program, as well as enough funds through the AmeriCorps grants to pay for 30 postgraduate credits. Upon completion of the six-week training, I embarked on my over 20-year career as a fully licensed elementary school educator with the NYC Department of Education – another example of the favor of God moving me from victim to victor.

I am humbled and awed at God's ability to move us into the good, despite our pasts, sometimes missing God's mark, seeming deficiencies and life's circumstances. I never thought I would be a teacher – tuition free, but this was part of the wonderful plan that God had for my life. "For I know the plans I have for you saith the Lord, not to harm you but to prosper you, give you peace and an expected end." (Jeremiah 29:11)

Academic Excellence and Self Worth

Through the vehicle of education and intellect I have found much of the self-worth that was needed to keep me believing, going forward, excelling and having something to be proud of in my life – that was the emotional function of intellect in my life. It brought my parents' approval, especially my mother's.

My parents were proud of me for all my academic accomplishments throughout my life. Sadly, I lived on their approval and thought that if I didn't have their approval – I didn't have their love. This notion – the notion that I was unwanted and something was wrong with me – stemmed from my birth. I unconsciously made the lie that there was something inherently wrong with me the reason for my mother abandoning me to adoption.

I subconsciously repeated this theme over and over in my mind throughout various painful moments, usually during relational breakups, abandonment, unfaithfulness and/or rejection. I lived for the approval of those I loved and did whatever I had to do to gain and never lose that approval. I was deathly afraid of emotional abandonment. I never felt enough. I always thought there was something wrong with me, that I had to earn love. I clung to academic excellence as the way to engender the approval and love of my parents.

This lie was buried deep within my heart – and I was only made aware of this notion as a mature woman. It took years for God's love to unravel and peel back this insidious onion layer. It was through

God's unconditional love that I received acceptance and love not for performance – but because I was God's child.

Once convinced of God's unconditional love, I had to constantly take the opposite thought "captive" by shutting the voice up and recognizing it as a falsehood. I verbally and mentally replaced it with the truth that the circumstances of my birth had nothing to do with me, but everything to with my birth parents' insufficiencies or problems. This is a constant battle because these falsehoods about me were deeply entrenched for so long.

The scripture that always helps me fight against these self-defeating, low self-esteem thoughts is that God says in his word "I am fearfully and wonderfully made." In addition, "I am the apple of His eye", "great are the sum of his thoughts towards me," and I am "God's workmanship."

God blessed me with a keen mind that tantalized and reflected constantly – but many times worked against me. I was in a constant state of self-judgment coupled with a prevailing guilt that would linger and condemn me (which had its roots in the child molestation that I had undergone.) Again, God's word would counteract the lie as I repeated it in my mind and out loud, "There is therefore no condemnation to them which are in Christ Jesus…" I really began to understand why God saved me at such a young age to begin the healing process left by the devastation of child molestation.

As I grew older – I found that education and intellect was not enough to answer the unanswerable questions in my soul like, "Why did my mother leave me and let me go?" There was still a gaping hole inside my heart and I had no self-worth – even after I accepted Christ at age 11. It was not until I was 55 years of age that I realized that this heart hunger would not be completely filled or satisfied through anyone or anything else – but Jesus – plain and simple.

I could not go back to the past and change anything. All I had was each moment today. And for each today of my life Jesus loved me,

Jesus wanted me and Jesus valued me. Jesus was the only "bread of life" that filled my holes and the quests of my soul. I was always searching and groping for love – for more, but I learned through many trials and tears that I would always come up empty and more disappointed to the point where I almost completely gave up that I would ever find fulfillment – until one day I laid my life on the line with God.

I said to God, "either you tell me what I need or why am I the way I am or else it makes no sense to believe in you." In God's utter faithfulness and caring he directed me to scripture, which said, to the man who is full honey is loathsome, but to the hungry even the bitter tastes sweet (Proverbs 27:7).

God revealed to me that my problem was a deep heart hunger that could only be filled by the bread of life – Jesus Christ. The next revelation that God gave me through another scripture was that he desired me to live in "Jerusalem" as he told Israel. I looked up the meaning of Jerusalem and it meant tranquility and peaceful habitations.

I realized that any person, place or thing that caused or resulted in inner turmoil, confusion or chaos was to be identified and avoided and became a measurement if the person, place or thing was from God or from Satan. I saw relationships that were to bring turmoil and my spirit would revolt against that spirit so we could never see eye-to-eye or live in peace.

In my quest for love, fulfillment, belonging and satisfaction, I had tried everything imaginable in my life to fill the hole, especially what I thought was pleasure, but actually was numbing or postponing the pain, whether "sex, drugs or rock and roll." But…I always came running back to God's awaiting arms – His embrace – His unconditional love.

It made me wonder, why did I run away from God so much in my lifetime just to come running back to him? But I realized desperate souls try desperate things and the desperation sometimes blinds us from

the love and light in front of us. In light of that, I found it amazingly wonderful that God took me back each and every time, just like the father of the prodigal son, God waited and watched down the road for me to come home. This is another reason why I am still a child of God. God won't let me go. He *won't* let me go.

Gratitude does not express the depth of what I feel at this moment as I write these words. God *never* let me go… God was with *me*. Despite my disobedience, rebellion, blatant disrespect and wanting my will to be done – God understood the "why" that lied beneath those behaviors, trauma and abuse – and went straight to my heart with his love.

God completely forgave me and threw all of my sins in the sea of forgetfulness – all because of the finished works of the Cross. And as one minister said, "little by little he taught me how to fight, fight and defeat what tried to kill me inside and go forward." But it took a long time for me to really believe that everything was forgiven and that my life was not just a series of consequences as payment for my sins. Freedom!

Jesus' shed blood for my sins was sufficient even over 2,000 years later. All I had to do was believe, not rely on my works or changing behaviors to give me favor with God. What manner of love is this? No revenge – just forgiveness, no punishment but discipline dripping with mercy all because of the finished works of Jesus Christ on the cross.

There is no other God, prophet or religion in history that can make this claim of unconditional love as demonstrated in Christ's death, burial and resurrection, not Buddha, not Mohammed, not Hari Krishna, Hinduism, Scientology, Mormonism or any cult or religion not based on Jesus Christ and Him crucified. No one in the history of the world besides Jesus Christ has died on a cross for anyone's sins. That is why I believe.

I have never met anyone who knew me so completely but still tells me, "I am the apple of his eye." It is this kind of love that has gradually increased my belief in God's words about me and my worth and value while changing those inner thoughts that judge my existence to the core. The truth that disputes lies is that God counts me worthy and valuable enough to send His son Jesus Christ to die for my sins – in my place.

So if God thinks so highly of me, how dare I think otherwise about myself despite any circumstance or hateful, manipulative person passing across my path? He died so I can be a victor, not a victim. I am a victor in Christ and so are you if you receive His sacrifice of love and let God's words of love take root in your heart.

As I begin to understand myself and God better, I have moved into a new place of peace, tranquility and rest, while I allow God to transform me delicately, compassionately, and intentionally, even with the occasional bumps on the Christian road. This has only been possible because there remains one theme that was prevalent throughout my entire life. I am a hopeless ball of abandonment, rejections, and abusive, regretful confusion without Christ as the center of my life and heart.

But in Christ I am loved, secure, serene, accepted, purposeful, creative, authentic and full of strength, endurance, perseverance, grace, love and joy. That is victory. The finished works of the cross, provided by Jesus, is my victory over every demonic force that had tried or will try to destroy me and my purpose for existence.

This is my story of God's love towards me as he moved and moves me from victimhood to victory! I am still His workmanship in progress, moving toward Jesus's likeness – God wants me to live in victory. I want that too for myself. Both God and I agree that victory is my destiny. I am the head not the tail. I am the righteousness of God through Christ. I am part of a priesthood and holy nation. I am the beloved. Because of who God is, I am. But most of all, I am loved and

that love will never be taken away because it lives deep inside my heart where Jesus lives.

What makes me a victor is not simply my lifetime achievements, accomplishments or overcoming habits or obstacles or even understanding every piece of my life, personality or soul. What makes me a victor today is the Lord Jesus Christ and our unending intimate relationship that we've shared for over 45 years.

Jesus has been there every second of my life from birth until now – even before I knew Him, He knew me. "Before I formed in the womb, I knew you." (Jeremiah 1:5) His love has gone where no man or woman has ever gone with me. God has heard every one of my prayers, my cries, my agony and my quest for joy and peace.

Jesus is the only one. Jesus has never disappointed me, deserted me or rejected me, despite all of the wrong turns I made in my life. I am so grateful that I have known such a complete, unconditional, forgiving, compassionate love in Christ Jesus. I know that "I survived" because Jesus lives inside of me.

Because of the finished work of the cross – I can live in victory, in freedom, in wholeness, in strength, in self-acceptance and true authenticity – if I choose. Or I can live in the darkness of rebellion and die in more ways than one, as I have learned.

God, I thank you for this difficult but wonderful journey. I will always love you for your patience and kindness towards me yesterday, today, tomorrow and throughout eternity. My life is secure in you. I am no longer a victim of my past but finally a victor in my present and future. I have a new name. No longer is my name abused, rejected, shamed, abandoned and a fearful little girl.

I am a victorious, conquering, triumphant, overcoming, authentic woman who is, as you promised me that I would be, "a sharp threshing instrument having teeth, that I will beat the mountain small and turn them into chaff." (Isaiah 41:15) I am alive! I am a survivor!

I survived what could have permanently destroyed and killed me. I have become a strong, more confident, compassionate, creative, intelligent, force-to-be-reckoned with woman through all of these trials and tribulations. Because of your omnipotence and love I have been transformed from a victim to a Victor! It is all because of you, Lord. I am humbled and grateful. I look forward to even more transformation as I yield, submit and surrender to Your love drenched will.

Aging Parents Pandemic Survivor

While in the middle of my own struggles, I had to deal with the demise of both my parents as they succumbed to dementia. It was difficult functioning full time as an elementary school teacher by day and home health aide by evening and sometimes overnight and Sundays. I remember the days when both my mother and I ended up on the floor when I tried to transfer her from the wheelchair to her bed, and I had to call 911 for help.

Both of my parents lived until they were 95 years old, as dementia robbed them of their quality of life and eventually their existence. I cannot describe the helplessness I experienced as I watched each of them forget how to swallow, as I watched them slowly waste away. Through it all, I did my best to be their advocate and caregiver. Thank God for the wonderful help we had during the day, and eventually on weeknights until 8 p.m., so my mother could receive hospice care at home. But my father passed in a hospice facility, gasping for his last breath, the Tuesday after the devastating Hurricane Sandy in 2012.

During that caregiving season, I was experiencing chronic pain and mobility issues of my own. However, as an only child I can only lean on Jesus. I remember giving my mother her last dose of morphine a week after her birthday. While washing the dishes (the only thing I could control) I looked up and cried in desperation to God, "Why does my mother have to suffer to die?"

As I felt anger, fear and frustration rise, before it overtook me, I said to God, "I'm not trying to get angry and bitter, I just don't understand!" Two hours later the Lord took her home – a week after her 95th birthday in 2017. It was almost as if God was waiting for me to let go. You see, as an only child, I was very close to my parents and thought that I could never live without them and their love. But God got me through the pain, the tears, the uncertainty and I survived through letting them both go.

My heavenly father whispered in my ear, "I will never leave you or forsake you." Again, in the middle, I survived by God's love. Caregivers, take hope, you are not alone. God cares and he will be there through every moment – if you let him in.

"Leanness to Your Soul" - Pandemic Survivor

When Israel had their exodus out of Egypt, which represented slavery and bondage, God went with them on their journey through the wilderness to the Promised Land. However, Israel complained every step of the way, despite how God delivered them out of slavery, parted the Red Sea as they watched their oppressors drown; and God fed them manna from heaven, water from a rock, kept them from sickness, disease, even their shoes lasted for 40 years.

Like we do sometimes, Israel complained that it was not enough. They wanted more. God was angry with their ungrateful attitude after all his provisions, and Him answering their prayers in such a glorious manner. Israel left Egypt with all its wealth, gold, silver, precious stones and enough metal that they could build their spectacular, splendid temple once they reached the Promised Land. Israel began to miss Egypt, the place of their bondage, and longed for their "slave food."

They complained to Moses, enough of this manna from heaven. Imagine, "angel's food" wasn't good enough. Ungratefully, they snubbed their noses, like spoiled children, and ranted and raved for meat. God said "Ok, you want meat, I'll send so much meat until you vomit!" Soon after, quail began to arrive in the Israelites' camp, everywhere they looked quail and more quail. It wasn't raining men; it was raining quail! The bible says that God gave them what they wanted but sent "leanness" to their soul (Psalm 106:15).

Leanness can be defined as deficiency, inadequacy, meagerness – the opposite of abundance, fulfillment, and satisfaction – the delusion we think we will receive from contrary choices of self-sabotage, rebellious desperation and/or acute desire.

Surviving Our Choices...

Throughout this book, I have talked about the various pandemics that I have survived: rejection, abandonment, foster care, childhood incest, domestic violence, poverty, sexual, emotional and financial abuse – coupled with an "identify crisis."

However, some of those pandemics were worsened by personal choices, wants and insatiable desires. For example, each dangerous, toxic-unequal-insane-relationship with men was overwhelmingly an *unwanted* consequence of my choices. Unfortunately, many times I chose the forbidden, the off limits; excitement-filled-financial-users, those not connected to Christ, who lived in darkness – and loved it.

My choices were influenced by personal pain, loneliness, and fear, which led to rebellion and false identity. Tragically, *how* these men operated their lives was not based on kingdom principles of light, love, well-being and peace – but the ways of Satan's dark, selfish, destructive, "takers," narcissistic kingdom.

Attractive men – disguised as angels of light – sweet as sugar (until you are hooked) were predators and wolves in sheep's clothing. My former driving needs/desires/wants so blinded my common sense and wisdom that I ignored the "red flags" and made excuses for their lives and behavior. Consequently, God allowed me to have what *I* wanted – heart-hunger temporarily filled – but ultimately sent "leanness" to my soul.

But that time is OVER! I had to be honest with myself, take responsibility for my former choices. I reexamined what type of man I chose to love and allow to be a part of my life. I created a better profile of people, especially men, who would add value within the context of my authentic, healed, whole self and the plans and purposes God ordained and designed for my life and family.

This only occurred as I let God be the center of my heart – not a person, place or thing. Most importantly, I no longer beat myself up

with self-blame but lived in the joy of the beautiful new version God birthed out of the ashes. With new vigor I declared scriptures and CODA affirmations: "I am capable of change," "I deserve to be in relationships with equal partners" and the most precious, "I *am* a child of God."

I am sharing this as a warning – stop wasting your precious time and not-to-be-trifled-with-love! You are loved and too precious! Your life matters! Thankfully, it is not too late – you are alive and breathing – change is possible. It begins and ends with a realization that no one will ever love you as deeply and completely as God, *your* heavenly Father.

Even if you never had a father in your life, or an affirmative, attentive, non-abusive and "present" father – you do now! God is your heavenly Father who will never leave you or abandon you. Never! I am a living witness that a person can change, transform, transition and make better choices for their life. I have learned (and am still learning) how to live in "healthy sanity" – with intentional, respected, affirming boundaries – not prison bars. So can you – with Christ – you are not alone!

So, there is good news. In Romans 8:28, the apostle Paul tells all of us who have received Jesus Christ into our hearts, that despite our unwise, detrimental, rebellious choices, God is sovereign; God is compassionate; God has a plan for our lives that results in our good and His glory. We can survive the pandemic of "leanness to our soul." God promises, we can have confidence and declare, "For we know that all things work together for good, to them who love the Lord and are called according to his purpose."

There is hope, once we come clean, admit the truth to God and ourselves. We can even admit that we feel hopeless to change. We can repent, ask God for forgiveness and change our direction while holding God's *unchanging* hand. Insanity is doing the same thing over and over and expecting a different result.

I had to stop the insanity that was in my life. The truth is, God gave boundaries to protect me from evil men controlled by forces of darkness. When I rebelled against God's word, laws, commandments – boundaries to protect me – I found myself in harm's way. But that does not negate that no man had the right to put his hands on me or force me to have sex – despite my choices. God's love, grace, mercy and power pulled me out. This led me to honest self-reflection, repentance and extending forgiveness and love – to myself.

Hallelujah! Whoo-hoo! I became empowered to live in hope and given courage to tell my story – knowing my trauma is over – and does not define me. You can be free too! You can believe and know that abuse, mistakes, poor choices and negative words do not define you!

Enough said. Use this page as a point of self/life reflection and review the pandemics you survived. Remember it all *over*, you survived – you never have to live it again! Proactively, write down your feelings to get them out of your head and heart. (Note: A therapist or trained counselor can be helpful if some memories are too painful.)

This can be a tough question (invite the Holy Spirit into this process): "Is there any responsibility you need to take for your choices that have resulted in negative consequences, harm, hurt and/or pain?" Stop and reflect.

- Ask the Holy Spirit to come into your moment, into your reflection of your past and help you confront it and heal.
- Take out a writing instrument, paper, computer or cell phone and write. It's journal time!
- Write <u>whatever</u> the Holy Spirit brings to your mind.
- Now take that writing, hold it up to God, ask for forgiveness for your role in the drama and ask the Holy Spirit to help you change direction, heal and move forward.

- Note your triggers and responses, find new "go-tos" and more positive choices. Discover scriptures on that issue and begin to transform by the "renewing of your mind."
- Ask God for a Christian accountability partner to help you maintain your spiritual, mental and emotional sanity as you make better choices in the future.
- Be intentionally kind to yourself.
- Be careful how you talk about yourself. Your life and death is in the power of your tongue. Practice saying good, positive, affirming words about you and your life. When you are ready – speak to yourself in the mirror. The Bible is full of positive affirmations!

I am still in recovery from a past version of self and I'm confident that I can continue to evolve and make good choices. I believe the same for you. But it is up to *you* to believe that for yourself.

Love Recovered – Love Renewed

Lord, I thought love would be lost forever,
My insides hurt so bad…
But now I realize that the painful experiences of love,
Was part of my divine journey,
On the path prescribed by love.

Destination,
The true love of You.
The true love of me.
This love extending to others
through You
through me.

From out of the ruins, I arise,
Through the hurt and the doorway of pain, I walk,
Into the destiny predestined

before I was born, I live.

Love recovered – Love renewed
Love is You, Lord.
Love through me, Lord
To a hurting soul,
A soul caught in the grips of pain,
To embrace them with Your message of hope.

To alleviate their pain,
With Your love.
To dry their tears with Your Word,
That endures forever.

Only Your unconditional, unfailing,
everlasting, compassionate
love, grace and mercy,
Can mend the excruciating brokenness
of any human heart,
The torturous turmoil of any soul.

Love Recovered. Love Renewed.
Amen.

Family Love Victory

Joy In the Middle – Letters of Love

Dejshona – Daughter of Enlightenment

Dedicated

Eloquent

Justice

Sensitive

Honorable

Outstanding

Natural

Anointed

Michael – Like unto God

Majestic

Intentional

Challenging

High Standards

Anointed

Exquisite

Loyal

Matthew – Gift of God

Masterpiece

Anointed

Talented

Tenacious

Heartfelt

Engaging

Whimsical

Autumn's Coming...Autumn's Here!

I got the call in the wee hours
That the water was no longer in tact
Signaled that Autumn's coming…
She was about to break the barrier into this world!

We had been waiting for your arrival with anticipation
We looked forward to your birth
I was so excited to see a newborn again
without the labor just the joy!

I can't believe it!
I'm really going to be a grandmother…
a grandmother – me!

My virile son's beautiful wife
Has carried the holy seed of the next generation
to love and learn about the God
Of her father, grandmother and great grandmother
the divine legacy of three generations...

The God who formed her for nine months
and "knew her in her mother's womb"
It will be my joy as I read to her
the many wonderful stories about God and His love.

Throughout the book that will guide her life
– the Bible –
Lord. I dedicate Autumn to you today
I will do my part to point her to the Cross of Christ
So she can make Jesus her best friend
For a lifetime.

Thank you for this special gift
Right at this juncture in my life
The joy of Autumn's birth
took the grief of death away...

Now is time for celebration!
Dark clouds rolled away
Made room for the sunshine
Of a brand-new granddaughter-being-born day

The day is finally here!
We welcome you into both our families
Autumn
We waited with anticipation
Until we heard your first cry
Now we understand why
Autumn's in July!

Happy Birthday
Autumn!
Grandma loves you!

Bucket-List Victor

Most, if not all of us, have or had a special "bucket list" of experiences or accomplishments we hoped to complete in our lifetimes. We desired to experience the joy of the fulfillment of dreams, as we became "bucket-list" victors. Whether it was the completion of our education, becoming an author, starting a business or purchasing our first home – whatever – we all have/had dreams and hopes for ourselves. With each fulfilled dream, accomplishment and new beginning I realized I was living in the tomorrow I prayed for yesterday.

In the spaces below, list the special items on your bucket-list:

_____

_____

_____

_____

_____

_____

_____

_____

_____

_____

_____

_____

_____

_____

_____

_____

_____

_____

_____

_____

Published Victor

It took eight years for my first book, *"From the Heart, Poetry Birthed From the Altar of Life"* to be published. I felt like I was 11 months pregnant and could not deliver. Langston Hughes poem, "A Dream Deferred" echoed the anguish of my heart that turned into another poem on the road to victory and triumph. Similarly, *Pandemic Survivor: Victim to Victor* was also delayed and deferred.

God waited for me to experience his healing from two COVID-19 infections, survive, thrive, remotely teach, move into a co-op, have two major surgeries and retire in a pandemic: before publication! Ultimately, it took eight years for publication. Eight is the biblical number of new beginnings. God gave me another new beginning with publication of this book. Triumphantly and gratefully, I learned through the process that delay does not mean denial.

Dreams Deferred – Worth the Wait

What happens when your dreams don't happen?
When your hopes are not realized?
You feel powerless to bring real lasting change into your life.
Your visions and dreams became nightmares of
Unfulfilled disappointment…

Your job became a distraction
from the loneliness of a dream deferred,
A distraction from pain and purpose lost,
Disillusioned and disappointed,
The living room couch or recliner
Your soulmate,
The drone of media your solace.

Hope deferred.
Life deferred.
Dreams deferred.
As Langston Hughes in lyrically style,
"dried up like a raisin in the sun."
But…
A dream fulfilled is a sweet sudden sunrise
Only God can turn raisins back into grapes
Then process the grapes into fine wine.

Delay is not denial!
Delay teaches patience.
God's time makes victory and triumph
Even sweeter…
Smell the fragrance of dreams fulfilled
As you swish the wine in the sparkling crystal of time;
And savor the taste…
and smile.

Dream Fulfilled

I almost lost my job. Termination was looming and I became displaced. At the place of my reassignment as I awaited my hearing date, I met a woman author hoping to make a sale. With anticipation and a bounce of hope I asked, "Who was your publisher?" That question led to the delivery of the fruit inside that I waited eight long years to burst into this world.

Eight, the number of God's new beginnings. This was a new beginning for me. Less than three months later, on March 18, 2013, on my daughter's birthday, my first book was published, *From The Heart Poetry Birthed From the Altar of Life*. My lifelong dream fulfilled, "sweet sudden sunrise." Raisins turned into grapes, then wine and I smiled...

It was remarkable how God took me to the place of destiny through an adverse situation filled with injustice! What the enemy meant for evil, the annihilation of my career as a teacher, God used for good to position me for the last step in the publication of my life and testimony through poetry. God used negative circumstances, that I did not understand how anything good would be birthed from, to bring me into one of the greatest victories and triumphs of my life.

However, the crucial part of the victory was the journey – the highs and lows, the ebb and the flow – which were all necessary to make the victory even sweeter. This journey developed character, faith, patience and trust in God, as I experienced a seemingly crushing defeat, deferment, initial denial and momentary hopelessness.

The pain of an unfulfilled dream soon turned to the sweet wine of fulfillment. To add to triumph, about two months later I won the case, and my career bloomed until retirement in 2022 – eight years later! (Another new beginning!) Truly, the raisins transformed into grapes, seemingly impossible – but not for God.

I drank with joy and unmitigated gratitude the wine of God's promises fulfilled – another victory and triumph over the pandemic of detriment, deferment and waiting. Triumphantly, the Holy Spirit filled the "vaccine" with the "medicine" of hope and fulfillment. In effect, God "prepared a table before me in the presence of my enemies." On that table was my first published book.

Through the wilderness of this painstaking pandemic of deferment and delay something else was birthed along this journey. The journey qualified me, through personal experience, to speak words of encouragement to other struggling authors living in the land of publishing deferment and give tangible hope and a route to published success.

All you have to do is *start* writing and *do not give up* no matter what the opposition, obstacles or delay. God *will* birth the seed he planted – your book *will* be published – if you only begin and continue. Besides, you never know, your book may become a best seller! "For I know the plans I have for you saith the Lord, plans not to harm you but give you peace and an expected end." (Jeremiah 29:11) That expected end is always wrapped up in hope and faith.

Chronic Pain Pandemic Survivor and Authorship Victor

I learned an important truth through this season of chronic pain that has lasted about a decade. I am enduring the pain of recovery from total knee replacement and foot fusion surgery within seven months of each other, coupled with spinal stenosis, severe lumbar arthritis, a shoulder rotator cuff tendon tear and other issues. I learned that you cannot wait until healing and perfect conditions in your life to manifest – before you begin pursing your destiny.

We are living in the last days. Time is winding up before the church is raptured and our time to do things on this planet is over. Even if you do not believe in God or the rapture of the church, time is short! If there is one fact that we cannot deny during this pandemic is that tomorrow or even the next minute is not promised to any of us.

I lived in New York City, where multitudes of thousands were infected and died over the course of 6 months in 2020. Many of my friends and family members have been tragically impacted by COVID-19 and its variants. I endured infection twice and am grateful for life, health and strength.

I could not wait for perfect conditions to complete this book or to keep moving. I had to complete and publish this book facing severe pain and limited mobility each day. I worked on this book while in a wheelchair, walker and walking with a cane – if only a few feet. However, because God was with me and the hour is urgent, God chose now in the middle of all this adversity and infirmity to publish "Pandemic Survivor from Victim to Victor."

Why? Because the majority of us have to push through pain in order to survive and thrive. Only God can get the credit and glory for anything in my life. I wish I could say I did this all on my own, but that would be a lie. I have been able to accomplish completing and

publishing my second book and every other accomplishment in my life not because of my brilliance or talent but because of God, His power and will for my life.

If God is nudging you to start and begin your dream, do it now! Waiting when God says "Now!" is disobedience and dangerous. Tomorrow is not promised to you. God will help you push through every situation you face to accomplish His plans and purposes for your life – if you only believe, step out in faith and take risks.

The safest place to be is in the center of God's will, heart and love – even in a global pandemic! Whew! I just had to say that. It's all about faith. The time for excuses is over; they died with the pre-pandemic world. So, whatever your dream – your victory story begins with the first step – the step of faith. While in motion, God continued to heal. Currently, I only use a cane as the healing continues.

What is your first step? Good question, I'm glad you asked. If you do not know – just ask God for His will for your life. So, what did God tell, confirm or reveal to you? What is the first step you and God can take together towards destiny, purpose, victory and triumph? Once you receive an answer record it, in your phone, journal, notebook, piece of paper, laptop, computer or tablet.

Remember, "write the vision make it plain..." (Habakkuk 2:2) Also, remember this important point, whatever God's purpose(s) and destiny is it will always help or edify someone, be of service to the world or a certain demographic. God wants to bring light into dark places through us. Our purpose and destiny should not be motivated by selfish ambition but service in love. That is why I pray for God to search my heart and reveal to me – me. I rely on the Holy Spirit to daily search and ensure my motives and heart remain pure for kingdom effectiveness – not just platform.

Do not be deterred by present circumstances to embark on destiny. For example, in the middle of all I am going through, it looked like this book would die in the womb of my mind and never be

delivered into the world. However, God had the last say! This book was birthed. You are reading God's provision and purpose for my pain. God used this book to touch men and women's lives.

The trauma from my past (and present) had become a blueprint of healing for women and men decades later. What Jesus did for me, He is able, willing and waiting to do for you. Let God heal you and then share your journey – even as you heal – in a blog, podcast, post, TikTok, one-on-one conversations, movie, play, interview or even in a book.

I want to read your story! The world is waiting for your contribution. God saved you from utter destruction and death for a reason – as a pandemic survivor. Be committed to find out what that reason is. As the song declared, "You're alive because there's more…"

Small Business Victor

Enlightenment Now, LLC

That was the name of my first business. It began soon after I ended a hard-to-break-free toxic relationship in 2018 by God's power, love and grace. I always said I wanted to start my own business. One night, while eating dinner in a restaurant, I filled out an application on LegalZoom. I got stuck completing the on-line application and made a phone call the next day. With that one phone call – my business journey began. I conceived, and God delivered my first LLC.

The Holy Spirit began to download, as I was on the phone, the name and components of my business. It was amazing. Two weeks later, I received the official notice, the Articles of Organization and my first EIN number. While in an Uber on my way to a Missions Conference at my church, I received another download – the company's purpose. Enlightenment Now, LLC promoting "Education Equity."

That became the driving force fueling our educational services. Our company's goal was to use these exemplary services and provide academic excellence, information and opportunity to level the playing field for all children denied – especially underrepresented black and brown students. Providentially, I was able to share my story with fellow educators and administrators at education equity conferences regarding the education inequity and disparity I experienced.

The company was born out of the disparity and inequity that I faced as a public education student in America. During middle school, my guidance counsclor told us about our high school choices. We were offered only vocational high schools. I shared the news with my mother, who went to school the next day. She spoke to the principal and said, "How dare you only offer my daughter and her classmates

vocational high schools, when there are specialized high schools available!"

Just as my mother advocated for me, this company's mission is to "level the playing field" in education and continue her legacy of education advocacy. Enlightenment Now, LLC's mantra is "a quality education or access to information should not be dependent on a student's ZIP code." God used every part of my journey – even experiences of educational injustice, disparity and inequity to create a viable solution and bring hope and opportunity to many.

During the fall 2022 ASCD Education Equity Leadership Summit at National Harbor, I was given a unique opportunity. I was able to network with amazing education leaders from across the globe who continued to derive innovative ways to promote, measure and provide models of effective education with an eye on equity, raising awareness and tackling the realities of education disparity.

The "coasts" of my business were "enlarged" as I investigated the post-pandemic role of education consultants, technology and education equity officers. Reimagining and retooling businesses had become crucial during this "New Normal" pandemic reset. There was even a workshop on education branding which opened my mind to new possibilities and definitions of education and pedagogy.

Professionals shared their innovative ideas, as well as lessons learned in this pandemic and its impact on methods and premises of education. In addition, I had conversations with key individuals that steered me in the direction of publishing my third book surrounding issues of education equity/inequity in our country.

Ultimately, I was able to share pertinent reflective poetry (from my book) regarding observations of American political presidential milestones in racial equity and its impact on our students – resulting in book sales. (This too was accomplished using a cane to ambulate.) I could feel destiny and purpose surround me.

Only God knows what the future holds for Enlightenment Now, LLC as we promote education equity and raise awareness while providing pertinent information to families – especially in underrepresented communities.

Ownership Victor

Prospering in a Pandemic

*Renter-ship to Ownership Through The Threshold of a
New Beginning...The Move*

It took six long months. I endured the process: eligibility, documents required, waiting, more documents required and more waiting. Still, I was walking up steps and more steps to the third floor, holding back tears, wondering… when?

A 90-day closing journey took 180 days filled with twist, turns, emails, inspections, more emails and more waiting. My faith was stretched to the "Outer Limits" (Millennials should Google the 60s TV show of the same name.) I had to fight fear and keep hope, promise and trust alive in my heart. Each painful step-up multiple flights I said, in defiance of pain and waiting, "It won't be long, it won't be long!" as an excitement grew in my soul.

But I did not know when, I was waiting for when, when, when?! Finally, the date I prayed to God for moving was approaching. By faith, I prepared to move on Friday, December 18, 2020, without a date set for closing. I had no final word, no closing – no keys – just a promise and hope.

Still waiting, still believing, still dealing with mice – waiting for the answer to "when." But still I hung on, faith propelled me – "only one more week to promise realized," I told myself. I believed this in my heart – faith became evidence and substance – amazing!

Then God said, "Today."

Finally, I received the email that set the date for closing. It became real; this was really going to happen. I knew I was on the precipice – of a "New Beginning" – my exodus…as Donald Lawrence

sang. This was my exodus into my new Promised Land. This was the "land promised" that seemed so elusive as written in my poem "No Place For Me."

In purposefully serene peace I went to the bank, in the coronavirus pandemic, after remote teaching second grade in the Bronx. I walked down those flights of steps in victory, triumph and confidence – despite physical pain. I sat with the banker as I received the checks which represented miracle money saved for that purpose – a purpose now finally fulfilled. Surprisingly, neither the sellers nor their attorney showed at the closing – but the bank's representative was there. Triumphantly, I heard the most blessed words, "Congratulations on your new home!" spoken by the smiling bank representative. It was real; it was finished, God delivered on his promise. I became an owner – after four years of trial and "not yet." The past horror show was over – goodbye forever, mice, goodbye unmerciful steps, dirt, grime, substandard living, trash, gunshots, crime and strife.

It was official; I owned my first cooperative property. I had moved from renter-ship to ownership, during a pandemic, as a single woman over 50. Yes, I was at the precipice of a new beginning! I walked through my threshold into a new life, a new home, new address, and my new destination, the shores of my "Promised Land." This destiny was designed and implemented by God, as I stood and gazed with gratitude through my amazing new terrace sliding doors, looking at the Manhattan skyline lit up like a Christmas tree that evening. I will never forget that awesome feeling and experience of promise and hope fulfilled.

Pushed Through the Snow

"No weapon formed against me shall prosper…" (Isaiah 54:17)

I moved into destiny. I moved into my land promised – but not without obstacles. A severe snowstorm threatened to prevent the moving date. So, I prayed to God, "What should I do- wait or move?"

~ 112 ~

I had to make another destiny decision, by faith, and once again step past my comfort zone. "Yes, we will move," I told the movers, who said, "It's up to you."

The moment arrived on God's calendar of my life. I moved Friday morning December 18, 2020 – with snow and drifts everywhere. I could have waited until Monday, but there was something about moving by faith on that date. I could not have accomplished it alone; God controlled the weather. I trusted God – even in the face of uncertainty, which in the past was so hard to do.

I learned that sometimes you have to push through the snow and be uncomfortable to reach your destiny, your Promised Land, your next. It will never be a-walk-in-the-park, but many times a push-through-the-snow by faith in a God bigger, higher and more powerful than you. I met another obstacle to ownership and pushed through like a football player on the line, like a gazelle, I leapt over each hurdle in the race towards "It is finished!" I pushed through and jumped over to 'Next." I could see God smiling at my joy that He created.

Moving day happened the day after a blizzard. There were so many divine interventions that day! There was a cleared out protected parking space with barriers saved for the movers to park and pack the U-Haul truck. The U-Haul never got stuck in the snow, while we saw abandoned vehicles all over the snow filled streets. I had help to pack and move; all my important pieces fit in the truck on our way, and unnecessary items were parked on the snow filled sidewalk.

It was over. I was out of the wilderness into my destiny. Never to return to the past – closed the door behind me – I said my last goodbye. This assignment was over and the painful memories of a toxic loveless, Leah relationship – also left behind. Next assignment – New Beginnings. We were almost there – no longer a dream deferred – but fulfilled!

The Threshold

I was at destiny's door – waiting for the key at hand. I took the elevator for the first time to the "penthouse suite" prepared for me "before the foundations of the world." Six months of waiting, hurdles, obstacles, frustration finally over but not before producing "patience" fruit. I moved into the home that was already mine before I put the key in the door.

I took my first steps into the destiny God wanted for me. Into the home God wanted for his precious daughter – my soul rejoiced in gratitude. I sighed with contentment, accomplishment and winning the race – I crossed over into triumph. The only word to describe that moment – Joy! I walked through the threshold of my new beginning holding God's hand. My son Michael (my real estate agent) smiled and was just as excited that his mother was in her new home as he looked out the window at my amazing view.

The View

I sat down in my new living room, by the door of my new terrace, near my new dining room and I was captured by the view out of my new sliding window doors. I saw the amazing skyline of New York City, the white cotton clouds, blue sky and the light of the sun. I could see across the blue water the airplanes landing and taking off at LaGuardia Airport.

My new view. My new home. I was held captive by the beautiful view of my future only above, not below. In my former residence, on the third floor, I only viewed the streets, train station and projects – but now I see the view of my life as God sees me. God wanted me to see and soar with the eagles, clouds and blue sky. God wanted me to view only the present looking forward – not behind.

I closed the last door of my life to open God's door, which was waiting for me since the "foundations of the world." I was in the special home with the terrace I verbalized to God and desired – just for me. I

see myself through the view God showed me. I viewed my life through God's lens – as I gazed out the window at mesmerizing view. I declared out loud, "This is my home. The past is over. The future is today." Today, I was living in the future I prayed for yesterday.

New Beginnings.

I prayed for a new beginning for over eight years. There were times I felt I would be "stuck there" forever, as every prospect to move, to own, fell through. I almost began to stop hoping and just accept this life and home. But something inside would not die. I knew this stop was only temporary – not the end of the line.

Today I stand tall as I sit on the chair of my beautiful, uniquely elegant, yet modern dining room table as I type. I know in my heart that God has birthed a new beginning within me and without. Now my outsides match my insides – rejuvenated and renewed marvelously beautiful.

I celebrated my birthday and housewarming virtually at the same time on February 12, 2021, one month after recovering from COVID-19. Both were special and meaningful. Both were divinely aligned. I could have been dead from coronavirus, but God spared my life to celebrate another birthday and my new home.

I shared my testimony, my joy, the beauty of my temple that housed my spirit and the beauty of the new temple and home that housed me. Both divinely inspired, both bring glory to God, joy to me, and hope for others. My daughter, Dejshona, orchestrated the entire event, and my son, Michael, took an amazing picture that captured that special moment forever.

My daughter-in-law, Lori, attended the on-line event and my son, Matthew, called from Atlanta to wish me well. It was a great day to be alive and a great day to be me. The distraction of the pandemic did not prevent the joy of another birthday and housewarming. God

answered my prayers, my dreams and my hopes. I was not only a pandemic survivor, but thriver – fully alive!

My new beginning was the reality of my dream to own a home, publish another book, to move forward, to see the beauty and joy of life in and around me. My home wrapped me in a warm blanket of protection and care. When I woke up each morning, it was all still there – it was not a dream. God made reality of my dreams.

I embarked on my new beginning filled with health and healing for me and for others – all who God sends my way. For those who stood with me, beside me, believed, prayed and wanted the best for me. Additionally, my new beginning is a legacy for my children and future generations who have stepped over the threshold with me into my next and next and next. My new beginnings – repeated. This was not the end – but the beginning.

"In the Middle" Victor

"Victory In the Middle"

"Victory in the middle" is one of the most important concepts in this book. Many dreams die or become reality based on what happens in the middle. It is in the middle where the storms, difficulties, distractions and obstacles flourish.

The middle may look nothing like the finish line, the desired outcome, the book published, the business realized and profitable, you are speaking and encouraging thousands or whatever that dream, desire or outcome you have wanted for years. Passion, energy, faith and determination can die in the middle. There is a frustrating tension living in the "already but not yet." However, the middle does not have to be the end, or determine that your dream is over.

There is a sweet blessing in being a pandemic survivor of the middle. Not only surviving through the middle of the coronavirus pandemic – but the middle in our lives. I am an expert in surviving the middle. God showed me how to endure through tears and find moments of joy and contentment in the middle. I am still in the middle on some issues – but not hopeless or joyless.

You may ask, "How do you survive the middle?" You survive through faith, hope, surrender, trust – but most of all by not giving up – this is how you survive the middle. You have to believe there is "better" in and beyond the "middle." If you have given up hope for "better" – God has the power to impart faith, belief and hope. It only takes faith the size of a mustard seed – tiny faith – God will do the rest.

One day at a pain management doctor's office, I was writing while I waited. A woman reading over my shoulder said to me, "You should be a writer. Your poem talks about being in the middle. Many people write about end, the victory, the accomplishment – but most of us are in the middle." Her comment and the concept of victory in the

middle, identifying and celebrating each and every victory in the middle opened the eyes of my understanding. This new understanding caused a deep appreciation for each trial and difficulty I faced and survived. Thus, the poem featured in this book, "Shore Enough I Made It!" was born.

Similarly, you have survived and are surviving the middle until you reach your next summit. My word to you is do not give up! The middle will be your springboard to the next celebration and accomplishment until you reach your goals. There are valuable lessons for you to learn in the middle that are imperative as you reach the finish line and threshold to your "next."

It took eight years before my first book was published, in the middle of my father's death, my mother's blindness, career annihilation, a relationship ending, eviction, homelessness and third floor walk-up, bone-on-bone knees with fallen arches. But God!

Also, it took 18 years for me to complete and receive my B.A. in political science – full scholarships – but God! This victory occurred "in the middle" of poverty, on public assistance (5 years), as a single parent of twin infant boys and a seven-year-old girl. I pushed through with God's help.

Additionally, my first LLC was born after a horrendous break-up, severe pain, double digit weight loss, no sleep from grieving and anxiety. But God never left me. He brought joy back. It took many failed attempts – decades to own my first co-op. But by God's grace and provision – during a pandemic – I experienced ownership! Finally, I published my next book after two surgeries in the same year – while dealing with physical pain and difficulty. You can survive and thrive in the middle.

I learned, as TD Jakes shared in his book "Crushing," "Pressure turns to power when God does the pressing." Thank God Jesus was crushed and pressed but rose on the third day in triumph and now sits

at the right hand of the Father. Jesus forever demonstrated that I can be resurrected in victory and triumph – out of any adverse situation.

I have become a sweet wine that God and others can enjoy. However, it would not have come without adversity. As David, said, "It was good that I was afflicted." Now, I understand for the next time God wants to make a sweet new wine out of me. "Lord may I never forget the lessons of the wilderness." Selah…

Surgery/Rehab Pandemic Survivor
Victory in the Middle

I was born with flat feet that had become a serious problem when I reached my 50's. My arch had completely collapsed. By the age of 56, I had to wear custom-made orthotics. I experienced severe, relentless pain with each step – destroying my mobility and gait.

Finally, at 62 years old, I was able to have the four-hour surgery necessary to correct and create an arch. The surgeon had to make four incisions to realign bones, fuse bones, add screws, slice my heel and move it over 6 millimeters and lengthen my Achilles tendon – requiring another incision.

As you can imagine, this was quite an extensive surgery on my right foot. There was a six-month to year recovery period. The first 12 weeks were non-weight bearing, which created a catastrophic dilemma. I lived alone. Therefore, I had to go to the place I never wanted to go – a nursing home rehabilitation facility, especially in "the middle" of a pandemic. However, I knew that I was in the perfect will of God and I had to trust God with the uncertainty and unknowns.

The day after surgery, my surgeon said to me, "After I put the bones in place, an arch began to form." I immediately received a spiritual download. As I allowed the Holy Spirit to re-align my life, all that God had for my life would begin to form from nothing – but God's will. I realized that, like my foot, my life was going through re-alignment as God formed and fashioned me to resemble Christ.

However, there was a waiting process, a grueling waiting process as TD Jakes in his book "Crushing" calls it the "fermenting process." My Bishop, Carlton T. Brown called it the "marinating process." I was crushed by circumstance both physically and spiritually and now my natural and spiritual juices were waiting to "marinate" and "ferment" into "new wine" for the "new wineskins." But how was I to get around with only one foot that could touch the ground? For my safety, I was admitted into a subacute rehabilitation facility for a month. Fear gave way to hope as each day I grew stronger and learned how to live and thrive in my personal – "New Normal." Nothing looked the same, felt the same, or functioned the same. Everything was different and uncomfortable, but necessary for my ultimate healing.

Not only did I experience physical challenges with navigating my environment with one foot, but I simultaneously experienced digestive issues that would not quit. Ultimately, the digestive issues, (triggered by their food) beyond the foot surgery, thrust me out of the nursing home and I left.

I entered the threshold of my home into the next 'New Normal." I had to face being alone in my home with God, the Holy Spirit, Jesus, the Word of God, music, online church services, my walker, wheelchair, cell phone and faith. It took over two weeks to get services, including a home health aide, due to a national shortage I was told. The "pandemic" struck again! I had to change agencies twice. But God came through!

When man drops the ball – God picks it up. Various church friends and family visited, assisted, brought food and groceries. Just at the point – the breaking point – I found a home health aide, albeit private pay, but God provided. Even when everyone went home and I was alone, the love of God pulled me from the jaws of depression and despair.

Jesus was with me through every painful hop, on a bone-on-bone left knee, each struggle with an oversized wheelchair down

narrow hallways, when I was not able to get through the doorway of the bathroom or bedroom. I endured going from wheelchair to walker to get into the bathroom and bedroom, then hopped back to the wheelchair to get out. I was frustrated from getting stuck in the kitchen and hallways – as well as shoulder pain from overuse as I hopped using a walker.

But God gave me strength when I had none. All of this was coupled with the pain of surgical recovery. Once again, I was becoming a physical pain pandemic survivor. God supplied the grace I needed to deal with recovery pain and the healing process. Surprisingly, I grew stronger the more I was crushed, marinated and fermented. "All things worked together for my good" as I faced my fears. My faith and hope was renewed.

Our church's theme/goal for 2022 was "higher faith for a higher place." Well, God had stretched me beyond any point that I could imagine in my life. All of the excuses and victim mentality was confronted with each difficulty I faced. I heard the voices of internal conflict, "I can't do this," along with "Yes you can! You can do all things though Christ that strengthens you!" I yelled and cried at times but experienced the victory of doing what I previously thought I could not do. That was what God wanted me to learn – capability, endurance, faith, patience and perseverance.

Finally, I watched myself as I moved into serenity, acceptance, receiving God's love – completely at rest, at peace, confident and ultimately joyful. "For the joy set before me" – a brand new right foot and arch – Jesus taught me how to "endure my cross" – like he did. I saw how all of this recovery, suffering and overcoming obstacles had fit into God's perfect plan for my life.

Every single day the Holy Spirit and scripture pushed me to believe I could stand, move, walk and live my life with whatever support I needed to succeed. I learned to forget pride and live with "no

shame in my game" as I took each victorious step forward through Christ's strength – no matter how awkward I looked or felt.

As people watched God help me throughout each stage, their faith and hope increased in God's capacity, faithfulness and power to help them endure and move forward, just as I had.

It was during my recovery from both surgeries that I appreciated the new home that God gave me – again and again! Everything could have been worse. I could have recovered in a third-floor walk-up, in crowded conditions, with miniscule light and no terrace. Just imagine, a wheelchair up and down a staircase or hopping with a walker or crutches on the flights of stairs. Even in the wilderness of recovery God provided "pools, springs and rivers" – my home, my view, my family, friends, food, ZOOM church services, music, scriptures, prayer conference calls, eventually a home health aide and most importantly His love and presence, daily.

It was in the middle of recovery that I completed this book, had speaking engagements, traveled and lived! In life, we will experience so many different things, good and bad. Certain experiences require more faith than others. However, if we believe in God and hold His hand, He will take us through each and every one.

What I have learned in my 62 years is that I am not alone. God has helped me each step of the way. In the nursing home, I had the privilege of leading an 85-year-old woman to Christ, which was the highlight of that stay. Additionally, the day before I was leaving, I met another woman who shared the miracle of her "straight leg" that she never had – due to cerebral palsy. As I listened to the courage, humility and fortitude of that precious woman, I realized that I had so much to be thankful for and that I had no excuse but to try and push myself to the limit, as she – with so much less – had victoriously managed to do.

Walking in Victory

The beauty about walking with Jesus is you can move into the realm of victory in any situation. During my recovery, I was led into a new ministry – despite apprehension because of the level of commitment. I knew I was in a season of rest and recovery – but I found myself frequently drawn to prayer. I participated in ZOOM trainings for those interested in the intercessory prayer ministry.

In addition, from a hospital bed in a rehabilitation facility, I completed a ZOOM Bible study class on the life of Elijah. Thankfully, the class and intercessory prayer team helped me stay connected to God's Word, people from my local church and hope, refuting isolation. It was through these connections that I was encouraged, inspired and motivated to keep believing, seeking God, reading and listening to the Bible, all while in rehab and not walking.

I realized that although we were praying and interceding on behalf of others, leadership, ministries, members and families, the surrounding community, New York City, the nation and the world; we also prayed for each other. Therefore, I received support as well – especially when I returned home and faced new challenges.

The Interview

During my recovery, I was asked by a childhood friend who was a producer to be interviewed on the internet radio station, VEGE Radio, in 2022. He saw my Facebook post and photo holding my book for the Alumni Authors Collection at the Bronx High School of Science Library on Alumni Day June 12, 2022.

The interviewer asked questions on topics from my first book, *From the Heart Poetry Birthed from the Altar of Life*. Again, I realized the full relevancy of all the "pandemics" I survived. I accepted that my story provided valuable information for others survival and victory. God gave me an opportunity to boast on Him and how He brought me through every trauma and situation I experienced. It was my utmost privilege to use my gifts and talents for God's glory as I told my unique story.

Later, I was asked to do a podcast– since the interview was engaging – especially the conversations on domestic violence, systemic inequity and education. I marveled how God used those difficult, not-so-glorious-experiences as a source of encouragement and inspiration for others. In addition, I learned that *God* qualifies and equips us for our journeys, purposes and destinies.

Retirement Victor

*For we know that all things work together for good for them
who love the Lord who are the called according to his purpose.*
Romans 8:28

A Leap of Faith

Sometimes we have to take a leap of faith into the unknown. I took my leap on July 1, 2022, when I retired from teaching in the NYC Department of Education after more than 20 years. It was not an easy decision, with many considerations, but in the final analysis I knew in my heart that it was time to leave.

The main reason to retire at that point was to fully recover from two surgeries and back issues that had a negative impact on basic mobility. God used these issues as a door to walk through into the next season of my life. I had to fight the fear of loss of income and change. However, at this point in my life, God has taught me that my employment is not my source of survival, God is my source.

I learned that everything else is a resource that God used but that all of my sustenance and provision came from the LORD. I knew that there were more chapters in my life, even as I grew older. Nonetheless, my retirement was one of the greatest triumphs in my career. I "completed my course," despite all obstacles that threatened to annihilate my teaching career. I taught wonderful children from New York City, giving them the tools to be successful not only in academia, but in life, as I boosted their self-esteem along with their reading, math and science scores.

I felt honored, humbled and privileged that God entrusted me with his most precious gifts – children. Retirement is not an end but a new beginning, a door, a portal to the next season in our journey. I am excited about all the possibilities and the amazing "next" God had planned for me even "before the foundations of the world" as I walked

in providence. "I am not retired but refired!" I fully understand the frequent declaration of the late "Daddy" Leader, an amazing senior Elder who possessed the spirit of Caleb and continued to climb mountains for the kingdom of God. Despite his old age – God's fire of love burned brightly in his life. I prayed that God's fire of love would continue to burn brightly through me for the rest of my life as I touched others with the warmth of His love.

In conclusion, I am thankful for every storm as a teacher that God has brought me through. I know that Jesus walked with me through this open door called retirement. The enemy tried to annihilate my career as a teacher, but God, as always, had the last say so. God triumphantly brought me safely to the shores of my new beginning as I said good-bye to a wonderful career. I am a Retirement Victor moving into "Next."

Atlanta Victor

"Loosed to Evolve..."

As a result of being retired, I was able to travel during September – for the first time in over 20 years. Also, for the first time, I was able to attend the 2022 Women Thou Art Loosed (WTAL) Conference in Atlanta, Georgia. I prayed for this trip and conference to be a springboard to my next. God richly answered my heartfelt prayer.

The first day I landed was filled with destiny moments. I literally ran into my son Matthew at Metro Diner and we had a joyous reunion as we sang karaoke. At the same venue, I met an attendee of the Prosperity Now Summit for Economic Justice who invited me to attend their closing session. The next day I went and met a blessed professional woman (and deliverance minister) who spoke prophetically into my life and confirmed purpose, in a secular conference during lunch – *before* we had a conversation.

Later that evening at WTAL, I received numerous "spiritual downloads of instruction" from three anointed women speakers during

"Midnight Madness" – as the rafters shook with worship at 12 a.m. (like Paul and Silas). Previously, at another presentation at the hotel, I received a text from my publisher that my poetry book was ready for re-print (the former company was defunct) with a "new and improved" front cover, which was indicative of my "new and improved" life.

God was surely doing "a new thing" and yes, I did "perceive" it! However, I should not have been surprised, since the scripture guiding my church's Consecration Week for New Year's was God commanding us "to forget the former things" because He was "doing a new thing." (Isaiah 43:18-20)

However, I was still surprised, grateful and awed. I was living in the future that I prayed for yesterday. That future came all in God's perfect timing. After the crushing, fermenting, marinating, waiting and humbling – God said "Today!" Notice, victory arrived before surgical recovery had completed.

While I was walking wobbly with a cane and lumbar pain, God delivered me into my next. We must move with the cloud – when God says "Go!" – despite negative or imperfect circumstances – even if we have to travel alone. With each step, even if I had to rest, God proved that His grace was sufficient for me. I lived and walked as "God's strength was made perfect in my weakness." (2 Corinthians 12:8-10)

I was able to share and market my book with various women throughout the week in hotels, resorts – even restaurants – wherever the Lord sent my feet. Each woman was excited for me and could not wait to dive into my poetry book, *From the Heart Poetry Birthed From The Altar of Life* (available on Amazon).

The enemy tried to thwart my trip to Atlanta with a lost passport and wallet, because he wanted to prevent a divine appointment that God had scheduled for me. Two days before my trip, I lost my wallet and passport. After prayer, encouragement from my daughter to look one more time – after endless searching – I recovered both in time for my

departure. The enemy hoped his tactics would prevent God's inevitable which was my arrival in Atlanta and fulfillment of purpose.

Providentially, I met another professional woman at the hotel restaurant, with whom I shared my poem, "Domestic Violence the Cycle Continues…" the story of the worst domestic violence trauma I had experienced while pregnant with my first child at 22.

She gasped, "I never thought I would read this in print!" I thought she meant a poem about domestic violence. Then she exclaimed, "This is my testimony!" When I was a child, I watched my mother's boyfriend kick her in her stomach when she was pregnant. I have had years of counseling as a result."

I was flabbergasted! This encounter seemed surreal! Who could imagine that our paths would cross during the *same* WTAL conference in Atlanta, at the *same* precise time, that I would share *this* specific poem with her and that she had experienced the *same* trauma I experienced almost four decades earlier?

Only God could have orchestrated that divine destiny moment! God used every painful experience in my past to bring hope, healing and comfort to women along my journey – through transparent poetry. It is true, "The steps of a righteous man (or woman) are ordered by the LORD." (Psalm 37:23) I realized, just as Sarah Jakes-Roberts declared, "I was loosed – to evolve" into the destiny and purposes that God created for *me*. Father, I stand in awe of you – Selah.

Domestic Violence Victor

"Life After Abuse – Survive and Thrive!"

Victory and triumph continued. All of a sudden, a whirlwind of opportunities became my "New Normal" as I shared my story of domestic violence survival, life after abuse, and poetry. Book sales increased exponentially while simultaneously I had the privilege of sharing hope with other survivors – as well as the public at large. Throughout October 2022, I gave presentations on "Breaking the Cycle of Domestic Violence," at Bronx Borough Hall, Iris House in Harlem, and the community hybrid event, "End the Silence!" I was asked to share at the Milagros Day Worldwide Survivors Open House.

Additionally, I received a special invitation for an event that featured domestic violence and cancer survivors and had an opportunity to read my poetry. To my surprise, I received the Faith Honoree plaque and a City Council Citation at this community event. Lastly, I shared at NORC's Elder Abuse, "Stop the Silence" presentation.

As this book ends, new chapters begin. I will continue to walk with God through the destiny thresholds of "New Beginnings." So can you!

In Conclusion...Self-Reflection

As our literary journey ends, I leave you with a few reflection considerations:

♦ For what destiny has God equipped *you*?

_____

_____

_____

♦ Who are *you* on the inside?

_____

_____

_____

♦ What skills, talents and abilities do *you* possess?

_____

_____

_____

♦ What would *you* do every day even if you did not receive payment?

_____

_____

_____

- What do *you* enjoy and do well?

_____

_____

_____

- What do *you* think is your purpose?

_____

_____

_____

- When will *you* get started on your dream(s)?

_____

_____

_____

- Have you created an action plan with dates and realistic goals?

_____

_____

_____

♦ With the aid of the Holy Spirit, through prayer, have a destiny conversation with God. Then write your next step(s) with a date as the Holy Spirit downloads.

_____

_____

_____

I hope this book has helped you realize or confirm *why* you survived all the pandemics of your life as you moved from Victim to Victor! Congratulations! You are alive and survived! Now thrive!

Epilogue

The world is waiting for your contribution as you discover and live in your purpose and divine destiny. We are all in this together, and we need each other. Draw closer to those that love you and that you love – as you move even deeper into God's loving arms. You, too, can do the impossible, as it says in Philippians 4:13, "I can do all things through Christ that strengthens me!" With God as our Captain and Admiral, all of us can sail on the sea of life into our unique destinies – for His glory! This is not the end – but a New Beginning!

The Beginning...

Shore Enough I Made It!

For decades of my life,
I've been swimming.
Many times just able to tread the waters
of turmoil, hurt, pain, disappointment, abuse,
discouragement, frustration, loneliness,
guilt and shame.

The tumultuous billows and waves
Threatened my existence – every day
At times I thought I would hopelessly drown,
in the seas of self-pity and codependency,
Or destroyed by self-destruction...

Because of excruciating pain.
But despite the destructive waves
Despite the danger,
Despite the sharks,
I swam, I swam...
And when exhausted, wearied and could not
in my humanness swim any more,
I was pulled to shore by a Divine force

Pulled to shore,
Floating on the broken pieces of my life;
But I survived.
Shore enough -
I made it!
I made it safely to the shore
of My Promised Land.

Today,
I'm exhausted, I'm broken,

I'm in pain, but I'm alive,
I'm grateful, sooo grateful
That the boisterous waves
did not become my premature grave…

I'm alive. I survived.
To see the light of a brand-New Day!
Shore enough – I made it!

As I got up,
I lifted up my head
from the soggy sand of my shore,
I stood up on arthritic knees and wobbly legs
Made feeble by the storms.
I lifted up my hands,

And with my voice parched by the sun and sea,
I cried, with a loud voice,
with tears in my eyes,
Thank you, Lord!
Thank you, God!
You guided me safely all the way,
Safely to the shore
Shore enough – I made it!

On the shore today I stand.
Today I walk,
While holding…
No, clinging to God's loving,
Strong, compassionate hand.
He promised to never let go.
And now those proven words my heart, soul and life
knew and forever knows -
God *never* let *me* go.

So I never gave up!
My Higher Power,
Alpha and Omega,
Still holds my hand,
As we walk on the beach of my, personal
Promised Land,
Of love, authenticity, hope, faith and trust.
No longer in the darkness of foreboding waves of
fear, guilt and shame.

As I gaze above,
With a wide, beautiful smile across my face,
The sky is blue.
When I look around,
I see the beautiful alabaster sand glistening,
and twinkling with the mica of hope.

The violent, destructive waves are far behind me
As I continue to walk forward.
Only the faint sound of the waves
Breaking on the rocks of the shore,
And the tide gently going in and out,
Whisper in my ears.

I'm walking on My Promised Land.
The milk and honey is delicious and nourishing.
It was well worth the wait, the hardships, the pain…
As God gave me the courage to face
What once gave me petrifying fear.
God has helped me deal with
as He healed
all the pain of my past,

Now lost in the sea of forgetfulness –
I have moved on!
God glued together all the broken pieces of my life
and created a beautiful, whole, blemish-less,
extraordinary, phenomenal
Best Me, I could be…
As I embrace my new freedom,
My new liberty,
I'm being mended more every day.

I embrace my new identity,
Once called broken – Tamar,
The glue of God's love made me whole.
My new name is Deborah,
Strong, Powerful, a
Phenomenal, Black, God Centered Woman,
Who walks in love,
Who walks in light…
Eleanor – Enlightenment!
Denise – Believer!
George – Cultivator!
I have fully accepted and believed my names,
As well as the names given me at birth,
Victoria – Victory!
Scott – Painted Warrior!

This is who I am.
This is my identity.
My names define me.
Now to forever walk in my authentic self.
Never to shrink anymore.
Never to bow my head down again.
It is finished! It is finished!
I hold my head high!

God has made me "a sharp threshing instrument
having teeth,
"To thresh the mountains
And beat them small."
I'm living in the season called
"Destiny!"
Whose open door beckons me to come in
To the city of Freedom,
The gates of Jerusalem.
Jerusalem filled with the meaning of its name,
"Tranquil Possessions" "Habitation of Peace."
Live in the depths of my heart.

I'm alive
and
All is well.

Shore enough - I made it!

Author's Note

If you would like to receive Jesus Christ into your heart and life and experience your spiritual "New Beginning" repeat this simple prayer:

"Dear Jesus, I believe that you love me and died for all my sins, hurt and pain. My God, I ask you to forgive me for my sins and come into my heart and life. I believe you are the Son of God and I want you to be the Lord and Savior of my life. Jesus, I want a New Beginning – with and in you. Fill me with your love, joy, peace and Holy Spirit. In Jesus' name I pray with thanksgiving – Amen."

If you prayed that prayer you are born-again or saved! Whoohoo! Welcome to the family of God! Ask the Holy Spirit to lead you to a Bible believing church with believers that can love, nurture and disciple you. You may also contact my church, Bethel Gospel Assembly, at bethelga.org or (212) 860-1510 for literature, prayer and New Believers classes for your new journey in Christ. Tell them Eleanor sent you! God Bless You!

Appendix

Scriptures to Heal the Hurt and Pain of Abandonment

The following poignant scriptures were also integral tools that have helped build my life and offset destruction and self-defeating patterns in my life. I pray these words will encourage and inspire you to have hope and take the first step towards transformation and victory!

Psalm 34:18 (ESV)

The LORD is near to the brokenhearted and saves the crushed in spirit.

Psalm 27:10 (ESV)

For my father and mother have forsaken me, but the LORD will take me in.

Deuteronomy 31:6 (ESV)

Be strong and courageous. Do not fear or be in dread of them, for it is the LORD your God who goes with you. He will not leave you or forsake you.

Joshua 1:9 (ESV)

...Do not be frightened, and do not be dismayed, for the LORD your God is with you wherever you go.

Romans 8:38-39 (ESV)

For I am sure that neither death nor life, nor angels nor rulers, nor things present nor things to come, nor powers, nor height nor depth, nor anything else in all creation, will be able to separate us from the love of God in Christ Jesus our Lord.

Isaiah 49:15-16 (ESV)

Can a woman forget her nursing child, that she should have no compassion on the son (or daughter) of her womb? Even these may forget, yet I will not forget you. Behold, I have engraved you on the palms of my hands; your walls are continually before me.

Jesus took on all of our abandonment, and he knew what it felt like to be abandoned. He is the only one in history who was abandoned by God while he hung on the cross with the sin of humanity on his shoulders. Unlike any human being, Jesus experienced being separated from His Father and felt the throngs of the worst abandonment in history as he cried on the cross:

Matthew 27:46 (ESV)

And about the ninth hour Jesus cried out with a loud voice, saying, "Eli, Eli, lema sabachthani?" that is "My God, my God, why have you forsaken me?"

2 Corinthians 5:27 (KJV)

Therefore if any man be in Christ, he is a new creature: old things are passed away; behold, all things are become new.

Philippians 4:13 (KJV)

I can do all things through Christ which strengthens me.

2 Timothy 1:7 (KJV)

For God hath not given us the spirit of fear; but of power, and of love and of a sound mind.

Victory...Is on the Horizon!

Look beyond your troubles
Look beyond your fears
You don't have to be discouraged
Let Jesus wipe away your tears
For just on the horizon
Victory is about to dawn
So get up and praise Him
Why be gloomy and forlorn?

For Jesus is the God of the brokenhearted
For crushed and broken spirits He came
So let Jesus into your heart and
Where you hurt
Let Him share and bear your pain
Jesus is touched with the feelings of our infirmities
His love and power will keep you sane.

Remember, victory is on the horizon
It's just beyond the dawn
Whatever the situation is
Trust Christ to pull you over the top
Of the hill you're destined to climb
You can see clearly
You can see the SONshine!

By Eleanor George

Acknowledgements

With gratitude in my heart, first I thank the Lord Jesus Christ for enabling me to write and communicate thoughts, emotions and a positive message of hope, as He created me to be a Victor! I also thank all of the wonderful people, family and friends who believed in God's talents, abilities, skills within me and His purposes for my life. You each have encouraged me to pursue and continue, no matter how difficult, as I share God's message of hope and unconditional love with the world. You are loved, from my heart.

About the Author

Eleanor D. George is a native New Yorker, who currently resides in the Bronx. She is the renowned author of *From the Heart: Poetry Birthed from the Altar of Life*. Ms. George is a thriving believer, a devoted mother of three adult children and a grandmother. She is a recently retired teacher, business owner and motivational/public speaker. Additionally, Ms. George is involved in the social justice ministry of Bethel Gospel Assembly in Harlem.

While raising her twin sons and daughter as a single parent on public assistance, Ms. George furthered her education. She earned a Master of Science in Education, Bachelor of Arts in Political Science and an Associate in Applied Science in Paralegal Studies/Lay Advocacy. She is the recipient of numerous awards, scholarships and fellowships and served as a New York City Teaching Fellow and Hunter College Public Service Scholar.

Despite many obstacles, Ms. George propelled forward with drive and tenacity to reach personal heights beyond reason. Jesus Christ remains the center of her life as she lives her mantra from Philippians 4:13, "I can do all things through Christ that strengthens me."

Ms. George encourages everyone she encounters through her books, motivational speaking and personal contact to become the phenomenal person God created them to be and to live their lives "intentionally on purpose!" Ms. George's life echoes down the echelons of time, "If I can do it – so can you! For with God nothing shall be impossible!"

CPSIA information can be obtained
at www.ICGtesting.com
Printed in the USA
JSHW070036260423
40773JS00009B/124